Better Homes Cookery

PARTIES and ENTERTAINING

Myra Street

COLLINS LONDON AND GLASGOW

Cover photograph by Roy Rich, Angel Studios

Contents

The secret of giving a really successful party is to prepare everything well in advance.

Unless you have an extra special memory it is essential to make lists of all ingredients, table arrangements, cutlery and linen required.

Such attention to detail bears out that, contrary to popular opinion, good parties rarely just happen—they are invariably well yet unobtrusively organised.

If you know that everything is prepared and ready, it is so much easier for you, the hostess, to enjoy yourself. Remember, if you are anxious it will be transferred to your guests and the party spirit will be dampened.

Do make sure that everything is well organised and all will run smoothly. Always cater within the limits of your kitchen and the space available for eating.

CHAPTER 1

Party Buffets

Buffet-type meals are the answer when you have less chairs and table space than can accommodate the number of guests you wish to invite.

There are several points to remember with this type of entertaining:

Food must be prepared in bite-sizes or slices . . . food which needs to be cut up by your guests is *out!*

Seats and cushions must be arranged on the floor as you can't expect people to eat a whole meal standing up.

Provide extra napkins in case of accidents——they usually happen!

Don't use your best cut glass for wine as this is the kind of party where people put the glasses anywhere.

Allow for conversation if you are serving several hot dishes—cold food which is meant to be hot is inexcusable.

"Do-It-Yourself" Dinner Party

Everything is prepared before the party and all you have to do when your guests arrive is look your best and spoil them with attention.

For 8 servings

MELON with ground ginger and caster sugar
BEEF BITES
    RAW MUSHROOM SALAD
    MIXED SALAD
    VINAIGRETTE SAUCE
LEMON or CHOCOLATE CHIFFON PIE

Mixed Salad

Beef Bites cooking in fondue dish.

Melon

Cut into required number of wedges, remove seeds. Cut the flesh away from the skin. Slice into pieces across the flesh and leave sitting on

8

the skin. You can save on forks by spearing the melon on cocktail sticks.

Beef Bites

1½ pounds fillet of beef, minced
1½ tablespoons tomato ketchup
1½ teaspoons horseradish
1½ teaspoons prepared mustard
1 small onion, minced
1 teaspoon salt
42 (¼ inch) cubes of cheddar cheese

Combine all the ingredients together, except cheese. Roll the mixture around the cheese cubes to form balls. Serve 6 balls to each guest. Provide fondue forks or bamboo skewers to allow your guests to cook the beef bites in a centrally placed fondue dish containing hot oil. (It is best to heat the fondue dish with oil on the stove and then transfer to the burner).

If you are feeling extravagant, allow six ounces fillet steak for each guest. Cut the fillet into 1 inch cubes and cook as for beef bites in the fondue dish.

Serve the following condiments with the beef bites or beef:

French Mustard	Barbecue Sauce
Horseradish Sauce	(see page 11)
Tomato Sauce	Mustard Pickle
	Curry Sauce

Mixed Salad

2 lettuces
4 tomatoes
2 sticks celery
1 small onion
1 small green pepper

Wash lettuce and tear into pieces. Cut tomatoes into small wedges. Slice celery and onion into rings. Deseed the pepper and chop into small pieces. Toss in vinaigrette.

Mushroom Salad

12 ounces mushrooms, sliced
watercress
vinaigrette sauce (without herbs)

Toss mushrooms in vinaigrette sauce and serve on a bed of watercress.

Vinaigrette Sauce

2 tablespoons wine vinegar
(or a mixture of wine and
lemon juice)
¼ teaspoon dry mustard
salt and pepper
6 tablespoons salad or olive oil
OPTIONAL:
1 tablespoon chopped green herbs
(parsley, chives, tarragon or basil)

Blend all ingredients in a screw-top jar and shake vigorously for 30 seconds. Add herbs just before dressing the salad.

Suggested Wines

For the main course, a robust red wine, e.g. Hungarian Bull's Blood, Spanish Rioja or Chianti.

If you prefer a choice of pie flavours serve one Chocolate Chiffon Pie and one Lemon Chiffon Pie.

Chocolate Chiffon Pie Filling

2 ounces unsweetened chocolate
¼ pint strong black coffee
1 dessertspoon powdered gelatine
1 dessertspoon cold water
3 egg yolks
4 ounces caster sugar
pinch of salt
¾ teaspoon vanilla essence
3 stiffly beaten egg whites
thick cream, whipped for decoration

Grate chocolate. Heat coffee. Melt chocolate in a bowl over hot water then add the coffee. Soak gelatine for 5 minutes in the cold water then add to coffee. Stir until dissolved. Beat egg yolks with half the sugar, stir in salt and vanilla essence and add to chocolate mixture. Stir and leave to cool. Beat egg whites stiffly, then beat remainder of sugar into egg whites. Fold into chocolate mixture. Turn into cold pastry case. Chill for 3-4 hours till set. Decorate with trails, roses or swirls of whipped cream.

Lemon Chiffon Pie

Make 2 pies for 8 servings

4 ounces rich short crust pastry
  (see below)
1 tablespoon gelatine
$\frac{1}{4}$ pint water
Juice of 3 lemons
Rind of 2 lemons
2 eggs, separated
3 ounces sugar
$\frac{1}{4}$ pint thick cream, whipped

Make sure that your bowl is completely dry and clean before whisking your egg whites. Fold the lemon mixture in carefully with a sharp edged tablespoon.

Pour into pastry shell with a spatula. Make a smooth surface to allow for decoration.

Line a pie plate or flan ring with the pastry. Prick the bottom and bake blind for 15 minutes at 400°F or Gas Mark 6. Remove baking beans and cook for a further 10 minutes. Allow to cool.

Dissolve gelatine in half the water. Put egg yolks, sugar, lemon juice and rind in a pan. Stir until thick over a gentle heat. Whisk egg whites until stiff. Add gelatine to cooled lemon mixture, add three-quarters of the cream and fold in egg whites. Pour into pastry shell and allow to chill in the refrigerator. Add remainder of whipped cream before serving.

RICH SHORT CRUST PASTRY

8 ounces plain flour
5 ounces butter or
  margarine
2 ounces caster sugar
1 egg yolk
pinch of salt
2-3 tablespoons water

Rub fat into salted, sieved flour until mixture is like fine breadcrumbs. Make a well in the centre of the mixture then add egg yolk and water. Knead lightly. Roll out to about $\frac{1}{8}$ inch thickness. Line flan ring or pie plate by lifting pastry on the rolling pin. It is then easily placed in position.
This will make 2 flans.

Lemon Chiffon Pie.

Chicken and Rice Buffet

PÂTÉ *For 8 servings*
TOAST FINGERS
FRIED CHICKEN
  BARBECUE SAUCE
  SAFFRON RICE
  FRENCH BEANS
  CORNBAKE
  RAW MIXED VEGETABLE SALAD
DANISH APPLECAKE
BANANA SOUFFLE

Pâté

2 ounces bacon, thinly sliced
2 tablespoons brandy
4 ounces calf's liver, minced
6 ounces chicken livers, coarsely
  chopped
1 egg
1 tablespoon cream
1 teaspoon lemon juice
½ clove garlic, crushed
salt and pepper

Line a pâté mould (the top of a Pyrex butter dish or small loaf tin is ideal) with bacon from which the rind has been cut. Sprinkle with a few drops of brandy. Mix the livers with the rest of the ingredients except the brandy. Heat the brandy in a ladle, set it alight and pour over the pâté. Cover with bacon and foil. Stand mould in a pan of water and cook in a slow oven (325°F or Gas Mark 2) for 1 hour. Remove from the oven and allow to cool. Chill overnight in the refrigerator. Turn out and garnish.

Fried Chicken

8 portions chicken
1 ounce flour
1 teaspoon paprika
pinch of salt
1 egg
white breadcrumbs
¼ pint cooking oil

Buffet table with Fried Chicken, Mixed Vegetable Salad and French Beans.

Rub chicken portions with lemon. Toss in flour, paprika and salt. Dip in beaten egg and coat with breadcrumbs. Heat oil until a cube of bread is fried an even golden brown then fry chicken, turning it until it is evenly browned and cooked.

Barbecue Sauce

½ ounce butter
1 onion, finely chopped
1 (15 ounce) can tomatoes
few drops of Tabasco sauce
salt and pepper
few drops of lemon juice
½ teaspoon sugar
2 tablespoons thin cream

Sauté onion in butter, add tomatoes, seasoning, lemon juice and sugar, simmer for 10-15 minutes. Sieve and add cream before serving.

Saffron Savoury Rice

1½ pounds long grained rice
1 medium onion, finely chopped
2 ounces butter
1½ pints chicken stock (made with
  stock cube)
salt and pepper
¼ teaspoon saffron

Melt butter in a casserole. Sweat the onions in the butter. Add the uncooked rice and stir until the grains are coated with butter. Add chicken stock, seasoning and saffron. Cover the casserole and bake in a moderate oven (350°F or Gas Mark 4) for about 30 minutes until the rice is tender.

Suggested Wine

One of the better red Burgundies, e.g. Volnay or a Pommard.

French Beans

2 pounds French beans
1 pound button onions
2 lettuce hearts
3 ounces butter
1 tablespoon sugar
chervil
salt

Wash and trim the beans. Peel the onions. Put the vegetables, butter, sugar, salt and ¼ pint water into a pan. Mix and bring to the boil. Add the chervil and cook covered over a low heat for ½ hour. Drain and add a knob of butter.

Mixed Vegetables

Cress
1 cucumber
4 young tomatoes
¼ pint vinaigrette sauce (see page 8)

Slice the vegetables and arrange them on a long or round dish in alternating rows, after dipping in the vinaigrette sauce.

Cornbake

2 cans corn
1 green pepper
salt and pepper
1 egg
¼ pint thin cream
1 ounce butter

Whisk egg and then stir in cream. Deseed pepper and chop into small pieces. Butter a casserole and arrange corn and pepper in the casserole. Sprinkle with salt and pepper, strain the cream and egg over the corn and pepper mixture. Dot with butter and bake in a warm oven 350°F or Gas Mark 3 for 15 minutes. Mark into portions when the cornbake comes out of the oven. Allow to cool slightly before removing from the tin otherwise the slices may break.

Either creamed corn or whole kernels can be used.

Banana Soufflé

3 eggs
3 ounces caster sugar
1 lemon
4 mashed bananas
scant ½ pint evaporated milk
¾ ounce powdered gelatine
3 tablespoons water
6 tablespoons thick cream
Rum or vanilla essence to taste
1 banana
9 ratafias

Separate yolks and whites of eggs. Grate lemon and squeeze the juice. Beat yolks with sugar, grated lemon rind and strained lemon juice over hot water until thick. Remove and cool. Stir in mashed bananas. Beat evaporated milk till frothy. Stir frothy evaporated milk into egg yolk mixture. Dissolve gelatine in water then add to the mixture. Lastly, fold in stiffly-beaten egg whites. Pour into a wet soufflé dish.

Decorate when set, with whipped cream sweetened and flavoured to taste with rum or vanilla, and with banana slices and ratafias.

Do not decorate too far in advance otherwise bananas will discolour. To prevent this dip banana slices in lemon juice.

Danish Apple Cake

1 pound cooking apples
8 ounces fresh breadcrumbs
8 ounces moist brown sugar
Redcurrant jelly
Thick cream, whipped

Spread the breadcrumbs on a baking tray, cover with sugar and dot with butter. Place in a moderate oven, 350°F or Gas Mark 4, turn frequently until the sugar is melted and the crumbs nicely browned. Meanwhile cut the apples and stew in a small amount of water. Liquidise or sieve. Arrange a layer of apples in a glass dish, cover with a thin layer of redcurrant jelly, then a layer of crumbs. Continue layers until all ingredients are used. Chill in the refrigerator and decorate with whipped cream and cherries.

Summer Buffet Lunch

CUCUMBER SOUP　　　*For 10 servings*
SALMON TROUT
　TOSSED SALAD (see page 8)
　POTATO SALAD
STRAWBERRIES WITH ORANGE
　CURAÇAO

Cucumber Soup

4 pounds cucumbers
1 pint water
salt and pepper
1 teaspoon summer savoury
½ pint thick cream
4 teaspoons tarragon
paprika

Cut about 20 thin slices of cucumber for garnish. Peel the remainder of the flesh and boil with seasoning and herbs for 20 minutes. Liquidise or sieve the mixture, cool and add cream. Chill and serve garnished with cucumber and parsley.

Poached Salmon Trout

1 (4-5 pound) salmon trout
COURT BOUILLON:
2 pints water (or dry white wine and water)
1 small carrot, peeled and sliced
1 small onion, peeled and sliced
1 small stalk of celery, washed and chopped
1 tablespoon lemon juice or vinegar
a few sprigs or parsley
1 bay leaf
4 peppercorns
2 level teaspoons salt

Put all ingredients in a pan and simmer for ½ hour. Allow to cool, strain before use. Clean the salmon and sprinkle the inside with fennel (optional), salt and pepper. Wrap in muslin, place on a rack in a large pan and pour in the *court bouillon*. Cook gently on a low heat, allowing 15 minutes for each pound. Allow to cool.

If you do not have a large saucepan improvise with two roasting tins, placing the fish on a grill rack and cook in a warm oven 325°F or Gas Mark 3.

The fish can be served as it is or coated in aspic and decorated with radishes, olives, tomatoes and sprigs or parsley.

Potato Salad

4 pounds potatoes
chives and parsley
1 pint mayonnaise (see page 18)

Boil the potatoes. Chop into slices. Season and sprinkle with chives and parsley. Mix with the mayonnaise.

Suggested Wines

A good Chablis with the fish and a light, refreshing Gewürztraminer with the strawberries.

Strawberries with Orange Curaçao

3½ pounds strawberries
6 oranges
3 tablespoons curaçao
1½ pounds caster sugar

Hull the strawberries, wash with cold water, sprinkle with sugar. Pile them on a serving dish. Squeeze four oranges and heat the juice over a low heat with the curaçao. Arrange slices of peeled orange around the strawberries and pour on juice.

Preparing Cucumber to garnish Soup

Cold Summer Buffet

WINE CUP　　　　　*For 8 servings*
GAZPACHO
GLAZED HAM
　MUSTARD SAUCE
　DUCHESSE POTATOES
　PEACH RING
　ROLLS (see page 24)
ICE CREAM CAKE

Wine Cup

1 bottle claret
1½ bottles vintage cider
1 bottle champagne cider
juice of 1 orange
¾ pint soda water
2 tablespoons Cointreau or Kirsch
sliced orange and lemon to decorate

Mix claret, cider, juice and liqueur in a bowl and chill for 1 hour. Before serving, add ice-cubes and pour in champagne cider. Decorate with sliced fruit.

Gazpacho

(SPANISH COLD SOUP)
1 clove garlic
6 ripe tomatoes
1 onion
1 green pepper
1 cucumber
6 tablespoons olive oil
4 tablespoons lemon juice
salt and cayenne pepper
½ pint tomato juice
2 slices of bread, diced

Remove garlic and tomato skins. Cut into pieces removing tomato pips. Open pepper and remove seeds, peel onion then chop the pepper and onion finely. Remove crust from bread. Put all ingredients into an electric blender except salt and lemon juice. Pour into bowl and season to taste. Put in the refrigerator for several hours. If too thick add a little cold water. To serve: pour into chilled soup plates with a lump of ice in each. A bowl of finely chopped cucumber and tomato may be handed separately.

Glazed Ham

Baked Ham

1 (4-5 pound) baked ham
whole cloves
4 tablespoons brown sugar
1 teaspoon mustard
1 can beer

Soak ham overnight in water, then in beer and water for a further 2 hours. Make a dough of flour and water. Cover the ham with dough, dab crust with lard or brush with melted fat or oil. Cook in moderate oven, 350°F or Gas Mark 4, allowing 30 minutes per pound. Remove from oven and cool slightly. Remove ham from the crust and cover with a mixture of mustard and brown sugar. Press cloves into the scored fat and return to the oven for browning.

Mustard Sauce

6 tablespoons thick cream
1½ tablespoons prepared mustard
1 teaspoon horseradish sauce
salt and pepper

Whip up cream and mustard until almost thick, add horseradish sauce and seasoning. Sour cream can also be used for this.

Duchesse Potatoes

2½ pounds potatoes
3 ounces butter
2 eggs
6 tablespoons milk

Peel the potatoes and cook in boiling, salted water. Drain, mash thoroughly and sieve. Add butter, seasoning, eggs and milk. Pipe or pile with a spoon and fork on to a buttered baking sheet, brush with egg and bake in a hot oven, 400°F or Gas Mark 6, for 10-15 minutes.

Peach Ring

1 large tin peach halves
½ teaspoon whole cloves
1 (6 inch) stick cinnamon
salt
2 tablespoons gelatine
½ pint water
1 rosy apple, cut into wedges and steeped in lemon juice

Drain peaches, keep the juice and add water to make up 1 pint. Combine peach juice, spices and salt in a saucepan and simmer for 10 minutes. Remove from heat, sieve and dissolve gelatine in the juice. Pour half the gelatine mixture into a ring mould and allow to partially set. Arrange quartered peaches and slices of apple, pushing the fruit down into the gelatine. Pour over the remainder of the gelatine. Chill until firm. Unmould on a bed of lettuce, garnish with peaches.

Ice Cream Cake

Chocolate ice cream
3 egg yolks
2½ ounces caster sugar
½ pint milk
4 ounces plain chocolate
4 tablespoons thick cream (slightly whipped)

Beat egg yolk and sugar together with a small whisk, gradually pour on milk heated to just below boiling. Strain liquid into a clean saucepan and cook on very low heat until mixture is slightly thickened. (Test by coating the back of a spoon). Leave to cool. Melt chocolate in a bowl over a saucepan of boiling water. Stir egg mixture into chocolate then fold in cream. Pour into an ice-tray and put into refrigerator at its coldest setting. Allow chocolate ice to become firm but not solid in freezing compartment.

Strawberry or Raspberry Ice

1 (15 ounce) can strawberries or raspberries
juice of 1 lemon

Sieve or liquidise strawberries or raspberries. Add lemon juice. Pour into ice tray and refrigerate until firm but not solid. Stir occasionally.

Cream Filling

¼ pint thick cream (lightly whipped)
2 teaspoons chopped angelica
1 tablespoon chopped almonds
1 tablespoon sultanas
1 tablespoon glacé cherries, chopped

Chill a 1½ pint mould or pudding bowl. Line the sides and bottom with the firmed chocolate ice and then pack over this a layer of strawberry or raspberry ice. Fill the space left in the middle with the cream filling. Freeze until solid. Remove from the mould by passing the bowl under cold water. Cut in slices to serve.

If you have a small freezing compartment in your refrigerator, you can make the Ice Cream Cake in a small loaf tin.

Party Buffet

If you have lots of guests to entertain, a buffet table laden with enticing nibbles takes the pressure off the bar—which is the most expensive area of home entertaining. A well laid table will help the party spirit and the gorgeous peach torte—on page 19—can act as a centre piece in place of flowers or candles. If you decide to have candles, do try to place them safely on the table. A selection from the following recipes will help any party to swing!

CHICKEN VOL-AU-VENTS *For 20 servings*
MUSHROOM VOL-AU-VENTS
TOASTED CHEESE BOWLS WITH
   SHRIMP SALAD
CANAPÉS
COTTAGE CHEESE DIP
COCKTAIL SAUSAGE ROLLS
HAM AND ASPARAGUS ROLLS
BOWLS OF SALAD
STUFFED TOMATOES AND
   STUFFED EGGS
ALMOND PEACH TORTE
CRISPY CRUNCH BOWL
GRAPEFRUIT HEDGEHOGS
MULLED WINE

Chicken Vol-au-Vents
Here you see the Vol-au-Vents ready to be filled with sauce.

Puff Pastry

You can buy puff pastry ready to roll. However, it is much more satisfying to make your own.

   1 pound plain flour
   1 teaspoon salt
   1 pound butter, margarine or Spry Puff
   scant $\frac{1}{2}$ pint water
   few drops lemon juice (optional)

Sieve flour and salt into a bowl. Rub in one ounce of fat and mix with water to a firm dough. Soften fat and form into oblong cake. Roll out dough and place fat in the centre. Fold dough over fat up one-third and down one-third. Seal edges and roll out to three times the length with a lightly floured rolling pin. Fold up one-third, down one-third, sealing the edges with the rolling pin. Give the pastry one half turn and repeat process seven times in all. Rest in refrigerator or cool larder between every second rolling.

Chicken Vol-au-Vents
Mushroom Vol-au-Vents

   8 ounces puff pastry (for each type)
   1 pint white sauce
   salt and pepper
   4 ounces mushrooms, finely chopped
   1 portion chicken, fried or foil-baked

Roll puff pastry to $\frac{1}{4}$ inch thickness and cut 24 rings with a 2 inch cutter. Place 12 on a rinsed baking sheet and cut out remaining 12 with a 1 inch cutter. Brush bottom layer with water and stick rings on top. Cook small rings and use as lids. Brush over with egg and water and cook for 10 minutes in a hot oven, 425°F or Gas Mark 7. Remove centre of vol au vents to make more room for the filling. Dry off in the oven for a few minutes. This is especially important if you intend to store the pastry cases.
To fill see white sauce method, page 17.

Toasted Cheese Bowl

Toasted Cheese Bowl. Cut crust from top and sides of 1 unsliced loaf of bread. Make long horizontal slit 1 inch from bottom of loaf, extending to within 1 inch of other end.

Leaving 1 inch around all sides, cut a rectangle straight down from top to slit. Lift out. Place loaf on greased baking sheet.

Blend 4 tablespoons soft butter or margarine with 5 ounces sharp cheese spread. Spread over top, sides and inside of loaf. Bake at 400°F or Gas Mark 6 for 10-12 minutes. Fill with shrimp salad. To serve, spoon salad on to plates, then slice loaf. Makes 5 or 6 servings.

White Sauce

2 ounces butter
2 ounces flour
1 pint milk
salt and pepper

Melt butter in a saucepan, add flour and stir in until a roux is formed. Add warm milk gradually and mix with a small whisk (this way you are assured of a lump-free sauce). Season well and mix half the sauce thoroughly with the chopped chicken in a bowl. Add chopped mushrooms to remainder of the sauce and mix well over a low heat for a few minutes.

Heat the sauces and then fill the warmed vol-au-vents before the party. Pop into a hot oven before serving. Garnish the mushroom vol-au-vents with a sprig of parsley and the chicken vol-au-vents with a sprinkling of paprika.

Sausage Rolls

8 ounces puff pastry
12 ounces sausage meat

Roll out puff pastry $\frac{1}{8}$-inch thick. Roll sausage meat into 10-inch rolls. Place a roll of sausage meat on pastry, damping the pastry each side of the sausage. Fold pastry over sausage meat, cut along the roll of pastry and sausage. Knock up the sealed edge with a sharp knife and divide into $1\frac{1}{2}$-inch lengths. Brush with egg. Bake 10 minutes until golden brown in hot oven, 425°F or Gas Mark 7. Heat in the oven for a few minutes before serving.

Canapés

Canapés consist of a base made from small squares, rectangular, oval or round slices of bread. They are either fried in deep fat, sautéed in butter, toasted or spread with plain butter or a butter mixture. Shortly before serving, they are spread with various seasoned mixtures or covered with thinly sliced fish, meat, poultry or cheese, all cut to fit the bread. Canapés may be garnished with parsley, watercress, truffles, olives, mushrooms, pimento, hardboiled eggs or anchovies. They may be served hot or cold and you should allow 2 or 3 of any kind for each individual serving.

COTTAGE CHEESE DIP

12 ounces cottage cheese
$\frac{1}{4}$ pint water
1 small clove garlic, crushed
1 tablespoon mayonnaise
4 slices crisp bacon
(crumbled)

Mix the ingredients together over a gentle heat. Serve with carrot sticks or small crackers.

Shrimp Salad for 4 Toasted Cheese Bowls

2 lettuces, shredded
1 pound shrimps or prawns
(or tuna fish)
3 sticks celery, sliced
6 hardboiled eggs, chopped
20 stuffed olives, sliced
1 cucumber, diced
$\frac{3}{4}$ pint mayonnaise
2 lemons

Toss lettuce, cucumber, hardboiled eggs and celery in mayonnaise and fill the toasted cheese bowl. Arrange shrimps and olives on top. Garnish with wedges of lemon.

Mayonnaise

3 egg yolks
$\frac{3}{4}$ pint olive oil
salt and pepper
1 small tablespoon vinegar
1 teaspoon English mustard

Stir egg yolks with a whisk in a bowl with salt, pepper, mustard and half the vinegar. Add the oil drop by drop, then in a very thin stream as the sauce begins to bind, stirring vigorously. Add a few drops of vinegar from time to time together with the oil. Then add the remainder of the vinegar and continue to stir until all the oil has been used and the sauce is thick and smooth. Lemon juice may be used instead of vinegar. Always keep the oil at room temperature.

Top left: Cottage Cheese Dip

Bottom right: Toasted Cheese Bowl with Shrimp Salad

Lovely fresh cream Almond Peach Torte.
Top layer can be decorated with fruit and cream or left plain with roasted almonds as shown on front cover.

Stuffed Eggs.
Various fillings may be used for these.

Stuffed Tomatoes and Stuffed Eggs

6 medium sized tomatoes
6 eggs, hardboiled
1 teaspoon chives
3 tablespoons mayonnaise
salt and pepper
1 small jar caviare (optional)

Halve the tomatoes or cut into water lilies, halve the boiled eggs lengthwise. Remove the egg yolks leaving the white intact. Sieve the yolks and the insides of the tomatoes into a bowl. Mix with chives, mayonnaise and seasoning. Pipe back into tomatoes and eggs. Alternatively the eggs can be filled with caviare or imitation caviare to which a squeeze of lemon juice has been added.

Ham and Asparagus Rolls

12 large slices cooked ham
2 cans asparagus spears

Halve slices of ham and roll round a piece of asparagus. Secure with a cocktail stick, spearing with a pickled onion.

Grapefruit Hedgehogs

2 whole grapefruits
1 can pineapple chunks
24 cubes Cheshire cheese
24 grilled cocktail sausages
12 cocktail cherries
12 white cocktail onions
12 green cocktail onions
1 apple cut in cubes
48 cocktail sticks

Arrange the grapefruits on small saucers surrounded with parsley or cress. Put the above ingredients on cocktail sticks; for example: cheese and apple; pineapple and cheese; sausage and pineapple; cheese and cocktail onions. Stick the cocktail sticks with the food bites into the grapefruit so that you get a very spiky effect. This adds colour to your table.

Crispy Crunchy Bowl

Fill a bowl with snipped, crispy fried bacon, small pieces of tomato (skinned), cubes of Stilton and Caerphilly cheese and shreds of celery. Invite guests to dip in.

Almond Peach Torte

1 (16 ounce) can sliced peaches
1 (7 ounce) crushed pineapple
8 ounces plain flour
2 ounces almonds, finely chopped and toasted
1 ounce caster sugar
$\frac{1}{2}$ teaspoon salt
4 ounces butter or margarine
$\frac{3}{4}$ pint thick cream, whipped
2 ounces caster sugar
$\frac{1}{4}$ teaspoon almond essence

Drain fruit well and chill. Sieve flour into a bowl, add almonds, sugar and salt, cut in butter or margarine. Gradually add 6 tablespoons of water, form into a ball and divide into 3 parts. Roll out 8-inch and $\frac{1}{8}$-inch thick. Place on an ungreased baking sheet in a fairly hot oven, 375°F or Gas Mark 5, till golden brown. Cool. Set aside 8 peach slices. Chop up the remainder, whip the cream, add sugar and essence. Set aside $\frac{1}{3}$ in a piping bag or to decorate the top. Fold chopped peaches and crushed pineapple into remaining cream. Sandwich the torte together and decorate with remaining cream and peaches on top.

Mulled Wine

4 bottles wine (Claret)
1 bottle port
4 tablespoons sugar (white)
48-60 cloves
freshly ground nutmeg

Put cloves and nutmeg in 1 pint water. Bring to boil, simmer for $\frac{1}{2}$ hour. Heat wines together —do not boil. Strain water into wines. Add sugar.

Madeira Mull

1 large sweet orange
12 cloves
1 bottle Madeira
pinch of ground ginger
1 miniature bottle apricot brandy
sugar (optional)
$\frac{1}{4}$-$\frac{1}{2}$ pint boiling water

Stud the orange with cloves and bake for $\frac{1}{2}$ hour in a moderate oven. Heat the Madeira, ground ginger and apricot brandy until near boiling point with baked orange floating on top. Simmer gently, adding sugar if necessary. Just before serving add boiling water.
Yield 2 pints. For 20 servings allow $4\frac{1}{2}$ pints.

CHAPTER 2

Dinner Parties

A dinner party for a few friends is my favourite way of entertaining. There is nothing like good food and good wine for encouraging good conversation.

Allow plenty of time between courses and prepare as much as you can in advance. An attentive hostess should not be absent from the table too long—even though she is cook and maid at the same time!

MUSHROOM SOUP *For 8 servings*
DINNER ROLLS (see page 24)
CROWN ROAST OF LAMB
   APRICOT STUFFING
   BRUSSEL SPROUTS
   ROAST POTATOES
   ROAST ONIONS
   CREAMED POTATOES
MERINGUE PYRAMID PUDDING
ORANGE ICES

Mushroom Soup

12 ounces mushrooms
1 pint stock (or water and stock cube)
1 onion, sliced
2 ounces butter
2 ounces flour
$\frac{3}{4}$ pint milk
salt and pepper
6 tablespoons cream

Sauté onion in butter, add the washed mushrooms after they have been finely chopped. Next add the stock and seasoning, allow to simmer for 30 minutes and sieve. Melt butter in a saucepan and blend with flour to form a roux. Add milk gradually and allow to thicken, stirring all the time. Add mushroom purée and simmer for 10-15 minutes. Remove from heat and check seasoning. Add cream just before serving and garnish with cooked mushrooms.

Serve with home-made dinner rolls.

Suggested wine

A good Beaujolais-Villages.

Crown Roast of Lamb

2 sections best end, neck of lamb (14-16 chops)
1 medium tin apricot halves
seasoning
Stuffing:
1 tablespoon parsley
3 ounces fresh white breadcrumbs
4 ounces dried apricots, soaked overnight
1 small onion, finely chopped
finely grated rind of 1 lemon
juice of $\frac{1}{2}$ lemon
1 egg

Place crown roast in a large roasting tin, season and wrap a piece of foil or greaseproof paper round the top of each rib to prevent browning during cooking. Brush the whole joint with cooking fat. Finely chop the apricots and mix with breadcrumbs, onion, lemon juice and parsley. Add the egg and mix thoroughly. Remove any fat from the middle of the crown and pack in the mixture. Dot the stuffing with a little butter.

Cook in the centre of a fairly hot oven, 375°F or Gas Mark 5, for 1$\frac{1}{2}$ hours. Remove foil from the top of each rib and finish with a cutlet frill. Garnish with apricot halves.

Roast Onions

Peel the onions. Place in water and bring to the boil. Drain and arrange the onions round the roast and paint with oil or cooking fat.

Allow approximately 1 hour cooking time.

The roasting onions impart a delicious flavour to the gravy juice. Keep warm while gravy is being made.

Roast Potatoes

16 medium sized potatoes, peeled
1½ ounces cooking fat
salt

Arrange salted potatoes round the meat allowing at least one hour for cooking.

You may find it is impossible to cook both the onions and potatoes with the roast; in this case cook the vegetables below the meat in the oven. Allow a slightly longer cooking time.

Gravy

Remove the meat, onions and potatoes from roasting tin, pour away fat, allowing sediment to remain, leaving about 2 tablespoons of fat in the tin. Put tin on top of the heat and stir in 2 tablespoons flour, stir until frothy. Draw tin from the heat and add ½ pint cooking water from the sprouts and ¼ pint stock. Allow to reduce on the heat, check seasoning and colour and strain into gravy boat. If the gravy needs colouring I prefer a few drops soya sauce as this gives a better colour than browning.

Brussels Sprouts

3 pounds Brussel Sprouts
1 ounce butter

Wash and prepare sprouts, removing only the discoloured leaves. Soak in cold salt water for a few minutes. Make a small cross in the base of each sprout. Cook in boiling salted water for 7-15 minutes, depending on size. Drain and toss in melted butter.

Do not overcook the Brussel Sprouts or they will discolour and break down.

Creamed Potatoes

3 pounds potatoes, peeled
salt and pepper
1 ounce butter
6 tablespoons milk

Boil potatoes in salted water until cooked. Mash then add seasoning, butter and milk. Beat with a wooden spoon until light and fluffy.

Crown Roast of Lamb

For sweet serve oranges hot or cold

Meringue Pyramid Pudding

2 cans mandarin oranges
2 ounces butter
½ pint juice from oranges
4 level teaspoons custard powder
additional sugar to taste
4 egg yolks
4 egg whites
6 heaped tablespoons caster sugar

Drain oranges, saving juice (making up with water if necessary). Blend custard powder with juice, boil 3 minutes, stirring continuously, add butter and sugar if required. Remove, stir in beaten yolk, cook very gently 2-3 minutes. Remove, stir in fruit, place in medium-sized fire proof dish. Allow to cool.

Topping: Whisk egg whites very stiffly until mixture stands up in straight points when whisk is lifted up quickly. Add 1 heaped tablespoon sugar and beat until as stiff as before. Fold in remaining sugar. Put into forcing bag with large tube; pipe in pyramid shape over fruit (or, if preferred, shape with a spoon). Bake 30 minutes in very slow oven 290°F or Gas Mark 1, third shelf from top. Serve warm or cold.

Orange Ices

8 oranges
Orange water ice
juice of 6 large oranges
1 pound caster sugar
juice of ½ lemon

Grate the rind of 3 of the oranges before squeezing. Stir sugar, water and finely grated orange rind in a large saucepan over a low heat until the sugar dissolves. Bring to the boil and cook rapidly for 10 minutes. Allow pan to cool. Add the juice from the oranges and lemon. Strain into two small ice trays and freeze until firm. Stir occasionally.

Slice the tops from the oranges and scoop out all the flesh until the shell is clean. Use the flesh to make an orange sauce, or pie filling if strained.

Fill the oranges with orange water ice and freeze until frosty.

Dinner Rolls

Success with Yeast Cookery

Yeast is a living organism which only grows under the right conditions. Warmth is essential for yeast growth, therefore the ingredients and utensils should be kept warm to encourage growth. Yeast grows at a temperature up to 105°F so the temperature of the liquid and warm places for proving should be around blood heat.

If you warm your flour or try to raise the dough in an oven at a high temperature the yeast is killed and the dough will not rise.

Fresh yeast should be putty coloured, should crumble easily and have a sweet smell. If well wrapped, it may be stored in the refrigerator for several days. Dried yeast may be used instead but make sure you carefully follow the directions on the tin or packet. Dough should be handled firmly but not roughly. Too much handling results in heavy texture: not enough kneading gives a badly textured mixture. Always bake at the correct temperature.

When possible weigh the ingredients as accuracy gives the best results in yeast cookery. Don't leave your yeast mixture in a draught because it slows down the action. Don't add salt to the yeast as it impedes the action. Add the salt to the flour. Always use lukewarm liquid to mix the yeast as hot liquid will kill the action.

Terms used in Yeast Cookery

Spongy: the appearance of small bubbles on the surface of the mixture when you add yeast and sugar to the liquid.

Proving: allowing the dough to expand in a warm place.

Kneading: is an important part of yeast cookery and is best done with the heel of the hand using the finger tips to bring the mixture into shape.

Knocking back: kneading the dough back to its original size after proving. Allow plenty of space at the top of the bowl for the dough to rise.

Dough must be covered when rising or proving, with a clean tea towel or a polythene sheet. The dough may be left to rise in a refrigerator but this takes a long time. If you have an electric mixer with a dough hook remember to use the slow speed for kneading.

Dinner Rolls

3 pounds strong plain flour
3 teaspoons salt
½ ounce dried yeast (1 ounce fresh)
1 teaspoon sugar
1½ pints lukewarm milk and water
    mixed

Sieve flour and salt into a bowl and stand in a warm place until flour is warmed through (if you use the oven be very careful not to overheat).

Mix dried yeast as directed, add sugar and up to one-third of warmed liquid. Sprinkle top lightly with flour and allow to rise in a warm (not hot) place. When the sponge breaks through (bubbles appear) blend the yeast with the flour and the remaining liquid to make an elastic dough. Turn on to a floured board and knead well. This is a vital process in bread-making or in any yeast recipe. Use the heel of the hand, push the dough and then bring it back to shape with the finger tips. When the dough is smooth, return to the bowl, cover with a damp tea towel or polythene sheet and allow the dough to double its size.

Loaf

Knead and put half the mixture into a 2 pound loaf tin (warmed, greased and floured), allow to prove until dough has risen to the top of the tin. Bake in a very hot oven, 475°F or Gas Mark 8, for 15 minutes then a further 10 minutes in a hot oven, 400°F or Gas Mark 6. Remove from loaf tin and stand on oven shelf for 5 minutes to brown crust.

Put a baking tin with water in the bottom of the oven when cooking yeast mixtures.

Rolls

Roll out remaining dough and cut into fancy shapes as shown on the next page.

Dinner Rolls

Try making the fancy and festive dinner rolls shown on this page and you'll find that it's very little trouble. You can shape them up very quickly. Use the recipe on the previous page—then let these sketches be your guide to making rolls the easy way.

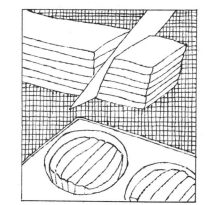

Fantans

Roll dough to a rectangle 14 inches wide and about $\frac{1}{4}$-inch thick. Cut across the width into $1\frac{1}{2}$-inch strips. Make a stack of 6 strips; cut into $1\frac{1}{2}$-inch squares, making 9 rolls. Place each roll, cut side down, in a greased patty tin.

Butterhorns

Roll dough to a 12-inch circle, about $\frac{1}{4}$-inch thick. Spread with softened butter or margarine. Cut into 12 pie-shaped wedges. Beginning at wide end of wedge, roll towards point. Arrange rolls, point side down, on baking sheet. For Crescents, slightly curve each roll.

Swirls

Roll dough to a 16 x 8-inch rectangle, about $\frac{1}{4}$-inch thick. Spread with softened butter or margarine. Top with cinnamon-sugar mixture or other filling. Beginning with the long side, roll up jelly roll fashion; seal seam. Slice into $1\frac{1}{2}$-inch sections. Place each, cut side down, in a greased patty tin.

Bowknots

Roll dough to a rectangle 8 inches wide and about $\frac{1}{2}$-inch thick. Cut across width into $\frac{3}{4}$-inch strips. Make 9-inch rope by rolling each strip back and forth under your fingers; tie *loosely* in a knot. Arrange on baking sheet. (For Rosettes, tuck ends under.)

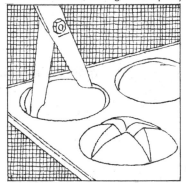

Shortcut Cloverleaves

Pinch off pieces of dough about the size of golf balls. Pull the edges of each piece down and under to form a smooth top; place in greased patty tin, one ball of dough to a cup. Snip across the top of each roll with scissors, making cuts at right angles to form cloverleaves.

Dinner Party

For 4 persons

CREME DUBARRY
BUTTERED TROUT
(or Trout with Cream Sauce)
STUFFED TOMATOES
SAUTÉ POTATOES
STRAWBERRY PANCAKES

Creme Dubarry

1 firm cauliflower
1 onion, roughly chopped
bay leaf
marjoram
1½ pints stock
seasoning and nutmeg
1½ ounces butter
1 ounce plain flour
¼ pint thin cream
1 egg yolk

Wash the cauliflower and steep in cold salt water for a few minutes. Retain some of the green leaves. Melt ½ ounce butter in a saucepan and sauté onion. Add stock and cauliflower with leaves, bay leaf and marjoram. Simmer for 30 minutes, remove cauliflower whole and drain. Retain 12 well-shaped florets and return the remaining florets to the soup. Simmer for a further 10 minutes. Sieve or liquidise. Melt butter in a saucepan, add flour to make a roux and gradually add the soup. Whisk together the cream and egg yolk. Add the cooled soup and reheat gently (without boiling) until the soup is thickened. Garnish with cauliflower florets.

Buttered Trout

4 trout
4 ounces butter
salt and pepper
lemon juice
fennel

Wash the trout, slit the bellies, sprinkle with salt, pepper, lemon juice and fennel. Place on a buttered dish. Spread softened butter over the trout. Cover with tin foil and bake in the oven, 350°F or Gas Mark 4, for 25 minutes.

Suggested wine
Try getting hold of a white Beaujolais—inexpensive and well worth searching for.

ALTERNATIVE:

Trout with Cream Sauce

4 trout
salt and pepper
juice of 1 lemon
½ pint thin cream
breadcrumbs

Arrange trout in a fireproof dish, add salt and pepper, the juice of 1 lemon and 4 tablespoons of water. Bake in a moderate oven, 375°F or Gas Mark 4, remove and drain. Put cooking liquor in a saucepan, stir in cream and reduce by half. Pour over trout. Sprinkle with breadcrumbs and brown in the oven.

Strawberry Pancakes.
Other fruits may be used in this recipe.

Sautéed Potatoes

2 pounds parboiled potatoes
4 ounces butter
1 teaspoon chives
1 tablespoon parsley

Cut potatoes in slices and sauté in butter, taking care not to break them. Chop the parsley and chives into remaining butter after the potatoes are cooked. Pour over before serving.

Stuffed Tomatoes

4 tomatoes
$1\frac{1}{2}$ ounces cooked rice
1 ounce slivered almonds
1 ounce butter
1 onion, finely chopped

Halve the tomatoes and remove the insides. Sauté the onion in the butter. Add almonds, cooked rice and tomato pulp. Season. Pile in the halved tomatoes. Dot each tomato with a little butter and bake in the oven for 15 minutes.

Strawberry Pancake

PANCAKE BATTER:
4 ounces plain flour
$\frac{1}{2}$ teaspoon salt
1 egg
$\frac{1}{2}$ pint milk
1 pound strawberries
1 ounce butter
juice of 2 oranges
rind of 1 orange
1 tablespoon icing sugar
2 tablespoons Grand Marnier

Make a well in the centre of the sieved flour and salt. Drop in the egg and a quarter of the milk. Beat until bubbles appear on the surface of the mixture. Carefully stir in the remaining milk. Allow to stand in a cool place for at least 1 hour. Grease an omelette pan or frying pan and allow to become thoroughly heated. Tip off excess fat and pour in enough batter for 1 pancake. Cover the bottom of the pan thinly with batter, turn over and allow the other side to cook. Pile one on top of another and cover with a cloth if not required immediately.

Heat 1 ounce of butter, the juice of the oranges and the rind in a frying pan. Add 1 tablespoon of icing sugar, mix well and add pancakes stuffed with strawberries. Pour in the heated Grand Marnier, flame and serve immediately.

Grilled Trout

Economical Dinner Parties

SOUSED HERRING
LAMB PROVENÇAL
  GREEN BEANS
CARAMEL CUSTARDS

For 4 servings

Soused Herring

4 herrings (filleted)
salt and peppercorns
1 onion, stuck with cloves
¼ pint vinegar
½ teaspoon tarragon
¼ pint water
1 bay leaf
1 level teaspoon salt

Cut off tails and fins. Season and roll up from head to tail. Place in an ovenproof dish. Simmer all the ingredients in a saucepan for 5 minutes and strain over the herring. Cover with foil or buttered paper. Bake in a warm oven, 325°F or Gas Mark 3, for 35-40 minutes. Allow to cool. Chill and serve with a lettuce leaf.

Lamb Provençal

1½ pounds New Zealand stewing lamb
1 carrot
2 large onions, sliced in rings
1 clove garlic
1 ounce butter
salt and freshly ground pepper
1 teaspoons lovage
½ pint stock
1 tablespoon tomato purée
3 large potatoes
chopped parsley

Dip the meat in seasoned flour and brown in butter. Place half in a buttered casserole. Sauté the garlic for a few minutes, together with the onions. Cover the meat in the casserole with some of the onions. Add a layer of sliced potatoes, season and sprinkle with lovage. Place the remaining meat, onion and potato in layers as before, finishing with a layer of potatoes. Pour the stock and tomato purée over the casserole, dot with butter, cover and bake in a warm oven, 325°F or Gas Mark 3, for 2½ hours. Raise the heat to 400°F, or Gas Mark 6. Remove the lid and brown the top potatoes.

Green Beans

1 (8 ounce) pack frozen beans
½ teaspoon summer savoury
1 ounce butter

Cook as directed on the pack but add summer savoury. Drain and toss in butter.

Caramel Custards

Caramel:
  3 ounces caster sugar
Custard:
  2 eggs
  2 egg yolks
  2 tablespoons sugar
  ¼ teaspoon vanilla essence
  1 pint milk

Put the caster sugar in a small saucepan and allow to melt without stirring. As it changes colour, stir carefully from time to time until it is a rich caramel colour. Warm 8 dariole moulds and coat the bottom with caramel.

Beat up eggs, sugar and vanilla in a bowl with a fork. Scald the milk and pour on to the eggs. Stir and pour into moulds. Stand in a roasting tin containing hot water, cover with buttered paper and put in a warm oven, 325°F or Gas Mark 3 until custard is set. Remove from the heat and allow to cool before turning out. Dip the bottom of the mould in boiling water to help the caramel out.

Young Tender Green Beans

FRENCH ONION SOUP *For 4 servings*
GRILLED MACKEREL
  RAVIGOTE SAUCE
  CARROTS AND PEAS À LA
  POLONAISE
  CHIPPED POTATOES
GOOSEBERRY FOOL

French Onion Soup

8 ounces onions
1½ ounces butter
½ ounce flour
1½ pints stock
seasoning
marjoram
bay leaf
slices of French bread
grated cheese

Slice onions and fry in melted butter until evenly browned but not too dark. Add flour and mix well. Pour the boiling stock over, season, add bay leaf and marjoram, and simmer for 30 minutes.

Butter slices of French bread, pile with cheese and bake for 10 minutes in a hot oven. Float the baked bread and cheese on the soup before serving—alternatively soup and bread can be baked in the oven together for 10 minutes before serving.

Grilled Mackerel

Season the mackerel fillets, brush with melted butter and grill. Serve with hot ravigote sauce.

Ravigote Sauce

10 tablespoons olive oil
4 tablespoons vinegar
½ teaspoon French mustard
1 small onion, finely chopped and pressed dry
1 tablespoon chopped parsley
1 teaspoon chervil
1 teaspoon tarragon
salt and pepper

Make up a *vinaigrette* with the oil, vinegar and mustard. Add all the other ingredients and heat gently.

Carrots à la Polonaise

1 pound carrots
2½ ounces butter
2 pounds fresh peas, cooked, or 1 packet frozen peas
6 tablespoons thick cream
paprika
salt and pepper

Choose fresh tender carrots. Peel them and cut them into little match sticks. Place them in a heavy saucepan with the butter and generous ¼ pint water. Season with salt, cover, and cook over a low heat for 45 minutes. Be sure that the water does not evaporate too quickly. If it seems to, lower the heat. Add the cooked or frozen peas well drained. Continue cooking until the peas are hot. The vegetables should be almost dry. Add the cream and heat, stirring constantly. Do not boil. Season with salt and pepper and a dash of paprika.

Chipped Potatoes

2 pounds chipped potatoes

Peel potatoes and cut into even-sized sticks. Heat fat and fry potatoes when the fat is hot enough to turn a cube of bread golden brown. When chips are cooked but not brown, remove the chip pasket, allow the fat to heat up again and return for a minute until the chips turn a pale golden brown. Drain well on a tissue.

Gooseberry Fool

1 pound gooseberries
3 tablespoons sugar
1½ level tablespoons custard powder
½ pint milk

Simmer fruit with water and then sieve. With tinned gooseberries just simply sieve.

Blend the custard powder with a little of the cold milk. Boil the remainder of the cold milk and pour over the custard mixture. Add 1 tablespoon sugar. When cool, beat together the fruit and custard and pour into individual glasses. Decorate with cherries and cream.

Steak Bake Oven Dinner

For 4 servings

AVOCADO AND GRAPEFRUIT SALAD
PORTERHOUSE STEAK
   SAUTÉED MUSHROOMS
   BAKED POTATOES
   MIXED SALAD (see page 8)
STRAWBERRY SUNSHINE

Avocado and Grapefruit Salad

1 lettuce
2 avocados
2 grapefruit
vinaigrette sauce (see page 8)

Put the whole grapefruit into boiling water and skin as for Florida Cocktail (see p. 80). Cut grapefruit into sections. Tear the lettuce and use to cover small individual plates. Arrange alternate slices of grapefruit with avocado. Serve with vinaigrette.

Porterhouse Steak

1 (2-3 pound) porterhouse steak
1 clove garlic, crushed
1 small onion, finely chopped
2 ounces butter
salt and pepper
Worcester Sauce

Slice the steak through the middle as you would a loaf of bread. Mix garlic, onion, seasoning and a few drops of Worcester sauce. Spread a layer of butter over each cut inner surface. Spread with onion mixture and sandwich together. Brown both outer edges in butter before wrapping in tin foil. Cook in a hot oven, 400°F or Gas Mark 4, for 45 minutes or longer for well done steak.

Suggested Wines

Nuits St. Georges or Chateauneuf-de-Pape.

Dividing the Porterhouse Steak

Strawberry Sunshine.
A variation on Baked Alaska.

Sautéed Mushrooms

8 ounces mushrooms
3 ounces butter

Slowly sauté the mushrooms in melted butter over a low heat. Serve with the steak.

Baked Potatoes

4 large or 8 medium potatoes
2 ounces butter
1 square of tin foil for each potato

Cut a cross on the top of each potato, smear with butter and salt, wrap in foil and bake in a moderate oven, 350°F or Gas Mark 4, until cooked—approx. $1\frac{1}{2}$ hours for large and 1 hour for medium.

Sour Cream and Chive Dressing

$\frac{1}{4}$ pint sour cream (or thin cream)
2 teaspoons chives
2 teaspoons parsley
salt and pepper

Finely chop the chives and parsley and add with seasoning to the cream.

Strawberry Sunshine

1 (8-inch) short crust pastry flan
baked blind (see page 9)
1 pound strawberries
2 teaspoons of arrowroot for
canned fruit
Lemon ice:
    juice of 2 lemons
    2 ounces caster sugar
    3 egg yolks
    $\frac{1}{4}$ pint cream

Make a custard in a double boiler with the lemon juice, sugar and egg yolks. Allow to cool, add cream. Freeze.

    Meringue:
    3 egg whites
    6 ounces caster sugar
    pinch of salt

Beat egg whites and salt until stiff and peaky. Add half of the sugar and beat until shiny. Fold in remaining sugar.
To complete Strawberry Sunshine proceed as follows. Put lemon ice in pastry case and cover with strawberries (if canned, previously thicken the juice with arrowroot). Pile on meringue and bake in a hot oven, 450°F or Gas Mark 8, for 5 minutes. Serve immediately.

A Dinner to Impress

For 4 servings

**ARTICHOKES AND HOLLANDAISE
  SAUCE
COQ AU VIN
  NEW POTATOES
  GREEN SALAD (see page 8)
RASPBERRY CREAM**

Whole Artichoke
Prepared Artichoke Heart

Artichokes and Hollandaise Sauce

4 artichokes
1 teaspoon salt
1 teaspoon olive oil
lemon juice

HOLLANDAISE SAUCE:
4 egg yolks
4 tablespoons water
1 teaspoon vinegar
4 peppercorns
8 ounces unsalted butter
lemon juice
salt and pepper

Cook the artichokes in boiling salted water, to which the oil and lemon juice has been added, for approximately 30 minutes. Serve whole with Hollandaise sauce handed separately. Pull off each leaf, dip the end in the sauce and eat with the fingers.
For the Hollandaise sauce, proceed as follows. Boil water, vinegar and peppercorns until reduced by half. Strain. Whisk the egg yolks with the liquid in a double boiler over simmering water. Gradually add the softened butter, whisking constantly. *Never boil the sauce.* Season with salt, pepper and lemon juice.

Coq au Vin

1 (3-3$\frac{1}{2}$ pound) chicken
2 ounces bacon
1 ounce butter
2 tablespoons olive oil
2 tablespoons flour
salt and freshly ground black pepper
2-3 cloves garlic, crushed
$\frac{1}{4}$ teaspoon thyme
$\frac{1}{4}$ teaspoon oregano
1 bay leaf
1 stalk parsley
12 button onions
12 mushrooms
4 tablespoons brandy
$\frac{1}{2}$ pint good red wine
1 tablespoon flour
$\frac{1}{2}$ ounce butter
chopped parsley

Melt the butter and add the oil. Cook the cubes of bacon until brown and crisp, then add onions and mushrooms. Sweat on a low heat until the onion is transparent. Remove and keep warm. Cut chicken into 4 pieces, toss in a polythene bag with the seasoned flour. Fry in the fat until chicken is golden brown. Put mushrooms, onions and bacon back into the casserole with the chicken; add seasoning, garlic and herbs. Cook until tender in a moderate oven, 350°F or Gas Mark 4.

I usually prepare this the night before since it is easier to remove the chicken pieces and skim off the fat after it is well cooled.

Heat casserole with skimmed juice until it is bubbling. Warm brandy, light and pour over the chicken. Allow to burn then add the red wine. Remove chicken and bubble the sauce until it is reduced by half, thicken with flour rubbed into butter. Strain. Return chicken and vegetables to a rinsed casserole, add sauce, cover and simmer in a very low oven until served. Sprinkle with finely chopped parsley just before serving.

New Potatoes

2 pounds new potatoes
2 ounces butter
salt and pepper
2 tablespoons chives

Scrape the skins off the new potatoes. *Do not peel them as this is wasteful,* Bring a pan of water up to the boil, add salt. Cook the potatoes until soft but do not allow them to break down. Drain the potatoes in a collander. Melt the butter in the saucepan, add chopped chives, then toss potatoes lightly in butter. Sprinkle with parsley before serving.

Preparation of heart of the artichoke

To cook bottoms, break off stem and lower leaves. Trim base with sharp knife. Cut top leaves $\frac{1}{2}$ inch above base. Scoop out choke; shape into cup. Rub with lemon juice. Cook in boiling water with small amount vinegar till tender.

Mouthwatering new potatoes being sprinkled with fresh parsley before serving.

Suggested Wine

St. Emilion—use the same wine for cooking the chicken.

Raspberry Cream

$\frac{1}{2}$ **pint thick cream**
2 tablespoons white wine
8 ounces raspberries
2 ounces caster sugar (if raspberries are fresh)

Wash and drain raspberries and cover with $1\frac{1}{2}$ ounces sugar. Whisk cream until thick, add remaining sugar then most of the raspberries— reserve a few for decoration. Arrange in individual glasses and chill.

This sweet can be made with any other fruit which you have available. However, if using canned fruit drain well as too much liquid makes the cream liquid.

The fruit and cream mixture can be alternated with ice cream and coloured jellies in tall glasses to make a Knickerbocker Glory.

Decorate with any of the following:
    Chopped cherries
    Chopped nuts
    Chocolate vermicelli
    Chocolate flake
    Crystallised orange or lemon slices.

B

A Non-Slave Dinner

For 4 servings

HOT SHERRIED CONSOMMÉ
CHEESE STRAWS
MUSHROOM SAUCE
PAMPERED BEEF STEAKS
JACKET POTATOES
  TOPPERS
TOSSED GREEN SALAD (see p. 8)
ICE CREAM & CHOCOLATE SAUCE

An extra-special dinner doesn't necessarily need hours and hours of toil over hot stoves. It can be one which you enjoy as much as your guests—like this one which features beef fillets done in an interesting and easy way. The meal starts off with tall goblets of hot Sherried Consommé and ends on a cool note—Ice Cream and Chocolate Sauce.

Hot Sherried Consommé

2 cans consommé (dilute as directed)
6 tablespoons dry sherry

Mix the consommé and sherry and heat slowly. Transfer to warmed serving dish. Serve in warmed wine goblets with cheese straws to the seated guests.

Cheese Straws

4 ounces plain flour
1 ounce butter
2 ounces grated cheese
1 egg yolk
1 tablespoon water
salt and cayenne pepper

Sieve flour and seasoning then rub in fat until the mixture resembles fine breadcrumbs. Add cheese and egg yolk, mix, then add water drop by drop until a stiff dough is obtained. Knead lightly. Roll out until thin and cut into narrow strips. Bake in a pre-heated oven, 400°F or Gas Mark 6, for about 7 minutes until golden brown. Small rings of pastry can be cut from the trimmings and cooked with the straws. Dip the ends of the straws into finely chopped parsley or paprika. Place a bundle of parsley through the rings. Serve one ring with each glass of Hot Sherried Consommé.

Pampered Beef Steaks

4 (1-inch thick) sirloin or fillet steaks
2 ounces butter
4 large mushroom caps
mushroom sauce
12 inch squares of thick tinfoil

Heat butter in a frying pan and brown steaks quickly on both sides. Place each steak on a piece of tinfoil, baste with mushroom sauce, place a buttered mushroom cap in the centre and fold the tinfoil to form a sealed packet. Place the packets on a roasting tin and cook for 20 minutes (30 minutes if required well done) in a pre-heated oven at 400°F or Gas Mark 6.

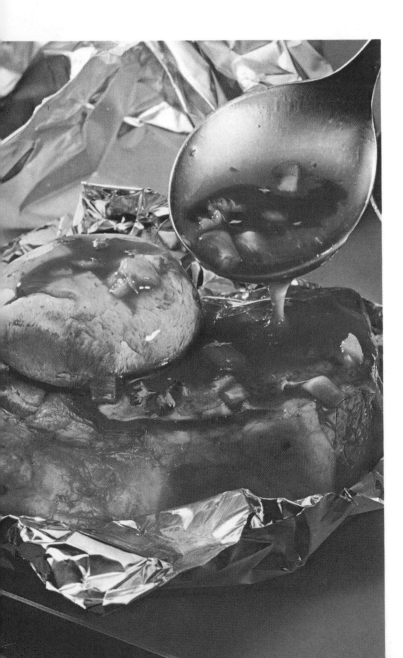

Basting the Pampered Beef Steaks and mushrooms with mushroom sauce.

Hot Sherried Consommé—a simple twist, a sensational effect!
Serve nippy cheese straws and thin saltines

Mushroom Sauce

4 ounces mushrooms, chopped
1 large onion, chopped
1 small green pepper, seeded and chopped
4 teaspoons cornflour
¼ pint burgundy
6 tablespoons water
2 tablespoons chopped parsley
salt and pepper

Add mushrooms, onion and green pepper to the fat remaining in the pan after the meat has been browned (see meat recipe). Cook until tender but not brown. Blend in the cornflour, add remaining ingredients, mix and allow to thicken.

Jacket Potatoes

1 large potato, scrubbed, per person

Cut a cross on the top of the potato and spread with a little butter. Sprinkle with salt. Wrap potato firmly in tinfoil. Cook in oven at 400°F or Gas Mark 6 for 1-1½ hours.

Toppers for Baked Potatoes

FOR EACH POTATO ALLOW:
1 portion cream cheese
¼ ounce butter
1 teaspoon chopped parsley
¼ teaspoon chives
a pinch of garlic salt
cayenne pepper

Cream the cheese and butter together then add the chives, parsley and seasoning. Top the potato with the mixture.

Ice Cream and Chocolate Sauce

1 large block ice cream
sauce:
    2 ounces dark chocolate
    ½ ounce butter
    flaked almonds

Stir butter into melted chocolate. Pour over the ice cream. Scatter with flaked almonds if you like.

Baked Potato

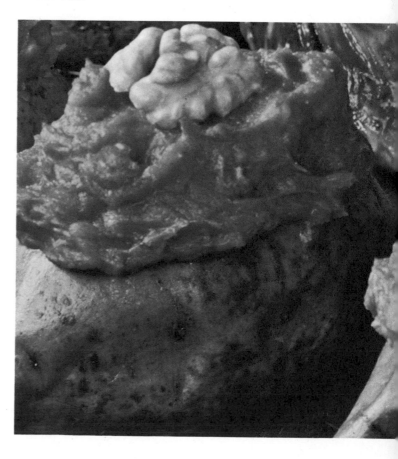

Early Closing Day Dinner

Have you noticed how often it is an early closing day for the shops when guests drop in for dinner at short notice? In such cases you have to depend on a small general store or greengrocer's shop which doesn't close. Here are two dinners which you can easily prepare on early closing days.

For 4 servings

TOMATO SOUP or MELON COCKTAIL
CHEESE SOUFFLÉ
　　SPINACH
　　SAUTÉED POTATOES (see p. 26)
FRUIT FLAN

Tomato Soup

　　1 large can tomato soup
　　½ onion
　　1 bay leaf
　　¼ teaspoon herbs
　　4 tablespoons single cream (or top of milk)
　　3 slices of bread

Heat the soup very slowly with herbs and onion.
Cut the bread into small cubes and fry in butter or deep fat until golden brown. Serve separately.
Put a tablespoon of cream into each soup bowl and strain in the soup.

Melon Cocktail

　　1 melon
　　1 can fruit cocktail

Prepare melon as shown, cut out flesh, dice and add to fruit cocktail. Return fruit to melon shell.

Cut a slice from the bottom of the melon to enable it to stand on a plate.

Cheese Soufflé

　　6 eggs (separated)
　　6 ounces grated cheese
　　1 ounce butter or margarine
　　1 ounce flour
　　scant ½ pint milk
　　¼ teaspoon mustard

Make a *roux* by stirring the flour into melted fat. Do not allow to brown. Make a smooth sauce by gradually adding heated milk. Stir in cheese, seasoning and mustard. When the mixture comes to the boil, remove from the heat. When the saucepan is cool enough for you to hold your hand against it, whisk in egg yolks one at a time. Whisk egg whites in a bowl until stiff then fold into the mixture. Pour into a greased soufflé dish and cook for 35 minutes in the middle of a moderate oven, 350°F or Gas Mark 4.

Spinach

Wash and remove stock from fresh spinach. Cook in a small amount of boiling salted water.
Cook frozen or canned spinach as directed.
Add a little cream before serving.

To prepare melon shell.
Thrust knife into centre at an angle; pull out. Make next cut at opposite angle. Repeat around melon.

Chocolate Fruit Flan

　　1 packet digestive biscuits
　　2 ounces plain chocolate
　　1 ounce margarine
　　1 tablespoon golden syrup

Place biscuits in a plastic bag and crush with a rolling pin. Melt chocolate over hot water, together with the margarine and syrup. Stir in biscuit crumbs and pack into a pie plate or flan ring. Firm in the refrigerator or a cool place. Fill with canned fruit; apricots or mandarin oranges are particularly good. Make up ¼ pint of the fruit juice with 2 level teaspoons of arrowroot and use for a glaze.

Cut four ¾-inch thick slices from a boneless, roll-shaped, ham. Brush each ham slice with oil or melted butter and grill for 5 minutes on each side with a gentle heat.

Drain canned pineapple slices, and use one for each ham slice. Cut the pineapple rings in half. Arrange two pieces at the end of a baking dish and overlap with ham slices.

Spread ham with marmalade. Cover the ovenproof dish and bake in the oven for 25 minutes at 350°F or Gas Mark 4.

If you are fortunate enough to have a delicatessen close at hand to help you out on early closing day, try the following menu.

For 6 servings
SHRIMP COCKTAIL
HAM SLICES WITH PINEAPPLE &
** MARMALADE GLAZE**
PEAS OR FRENCH BEANS
CREAMED POTATOES
ZABAGLIONE

Shrimp Cocktail

2 cans shrimps (8 ounces)
8 tablespoons mayonnaise
1 tablespoon tomato ketchup
1 lettuce
slices of cucumber
paprika
slices of lemon

Mix shrimps with mayonnaise and ketchup, arrange on torn lettuce leaves in a glass. Sprinkle with paprika and garnish with slice of cucumber and lemon.

Ham with Pineapple and Marmalade Glaze

Follow instructions shown in the left-hand column.

Creamed Potatoes

3 pounds potatoes
1 ounce butter
4 tablespoons milk
pepper and salt

Prepare as on page 23.

Peas or Beans

Cook as directed if frozen or freeze-dried. Pour over a little melted butter before serving.

Zabaglione

4 egg yolks
1½ ounces caster sugar
5 tablespoons sweet sherry
1 can fruit salad

Whisk egg yolks with a whisk until fluffy. Add sugar and sherry and beat the mixture over a double boiler until it is thick, creamy and leaves a trail. Put fruit in the bottom of the serving glasses and pour on the zabaglione.

Family Dinner

The two dinners included here have two things in common—they are the sort of meals where one invariably overeats and they involve a lot of washing up. In the family circle the eating pleasures can be uninhibited and, with a bit of luck, you can get the whole family in the kitchen afterwards to help with the washing up!

For 6 servings

SARDINE SALAD
ROAST BEEF
   YORKSHIRE PUDDING
   ROAST POTATOES
   CREAMED POTATOES
   ROAST PARSNIPS
   PEAS & CARROTS
   GRAVY
   HORSERADISH SAUCE & MUSTARD
PEACH CRUMBLE
   CREAM

Sardine Salad

2 cans sardines, drained
Vinaigrette dressing (see p. 8)
1 lettuce, washed and shredded
4 tomatoes, sliced
½ cucumber, sliced
6 baby beetroots

Arrange on individual plates.

Roast Beef

1 (3½ pound) sirloin roast

Rare: 15 minutes to the pound at 400°F or Gas Mark 6, and then 15 minutes to the pound at 325°F or Gas Mark 3.
Medium: 20 minutes to the pound at first temperature and then 20 minutes to the pound at second.
Well done: 25 minutes to the pound at first temperature and 25 minutes at second temperature. Preheat the oven and surround with evenly, thick-sliced salted potatoes and peeled parsnips with a little fat. Baste occasionally. When cooked, remove potatoes and keep warm. Pour excess fat into heated patty tins for the Yorkshire pudding.
For the gravy, add 1 teaspoon flour, salt and pepper, and ½ pint stock to the roasting tin. Stir over the heat. If no stock is available, use a beef cube and water. (see p. 23).

Yorkshire Pudding

8 ounces plain flour
1 teaspoon salt
2 eggs
1 pint milk

Make a well in the centre of the sieved flour and salt. Drop in eggs and half of the milk. Mix in the eggs and milk to obtain a thick batter. Beat until bubbles appear then add remaining milk, stirring gently. Leave the batter to stand in a cool place for an hour, if possible, before using. Pour into patty tins and cook for 10-15 minutes at 425°F or Gas Mark 7.

Peas and Carrots

Wash and scrape carrots. Cut into dice. Cook in a little boiling salted water for 10-15 minutes, until tender. Cook frozen or freeze-dried peas as directed and toss cooked peas and carrots together in melted butter with chopped parsley.

Creamed Potatoes (see p. 23)

Peach Crumble

1 large can peaches
4 tablespoons soft brown sugar
8 ounces plain flour
1 teaspoon cinnamon
½ teaspoon allspice
¼ teaspoon salt
6 ounces margarine or butter
2 tablespoons caster sugar

Butter an ovenproof dish and place peaches on bottom, leaving a few for decoration. Sprinkle with allspice and 2 tablespoons of brown sugar. Rub 5 ounces margarine into sieved flour, salt, cinnamon and caster sugar until mixture resembles fine breadcrumbs. Spread mixture on top of peaches, sprinkle with rest of brown sugar, dot with remaining ounce of margarine. Cook in moderate oven, 350°F or Gas Mark 4 for 25 minutes. Serve with cream.

OXTAIL SOUP   *For 6 servings*
ROAST CHICKEN
  STUFFING
  BACON ROLLS
  SWEET CORN
  ROAST POTATOES (see p. 23)
  CREAMED POTATOES (see p. 23)
  GRAVY (see p. 90)
PEACH MELBA

Oxtail Soup

2 pounds oxtail
2 onions
2 carrots
small piece of turnip
1½ ounces fat or dripping
2 ounces flour
¼ teaspoon marjoram
¼ teaspoon rosemary
¼ teaspoon basil
¼ teaspoon sage
pinch of thyme
1 bay leaf
salt and pepper
1 tablespoon tomato purée
6 tablespoons dry sherry
4½ pints stock or water

Cut the oxtail into 2-inch pieces. Blanch by putting in a saucepan of cold water, bring to the boil, remove from the heat and leave for 5 minutes. Remove the oxtail pieces, drain well and pat dry with tissue.
Melt fat or dripping in frying pan and brown oxtail, together with the coarsely chopped vegetables. Put into the soup pot and cook for a few minutes. Add stock or water, herbs and seasoning. Simmer for 2½-3 hours. Then add tomato paste and simmer for a further hour. Strain and leave stock for several hours so that fat can be skimmed from the top. Add sherry to stock before using, and garnish with meat cut out of the oxtail.

Roast Chicken

1 (3-4 pound) chicken
1½ ounces butter
2 rashers fat bacon
STUFFING:
1 medium chopped onion
2 ounces chopped chicken livers
4 ounces white breadcrumbs
1 teaspoon oregano
½ teaspoon sage
1 teaspoon parsley
salt and pepper
1 ounce melted butter
1 egg

Spread butter all over the chicken after mixing all the other ingredients together, except the bacon, stuff into the chicken. Cover the breast with bacon rashers and cover with tin foil (optional). Roast in a moderate oven, 350°F or Gas Mark 4, allowing 25 minutes to the pound and then another 25 minutes.
Make a gravy stock by boiling giblets with ¾ pint of water and an onion stuck with cloves. Boil until liquid is reduced by half.

Peach Melba

6 medium-sized peaches (or 12 canned halves)
1 block Vanilla ice cream
8 ounces raspberries
3 ounces icing sugar

For fresh peaches poach the peaches in fruit syrup (see page 88) without allowing them to get too soft. Cool in the syrup. Remove the skin and the kernel without damaging the fruit. Put the vanilla ice cream in a bowl or individual glasses and arrange the well drained peaches on top. Cover them with very cold raspberry purée made with the raspberries rubbed through a sieve and mixed with the icing sugar.

Peach Melba

CHAPTER 3

Supper Parties

Supper parties are an ideal way for the working woman to entertain friends during the week. Serve two courses which are easily prepared the night before. The table can be informally laid. Beer or cider accompanying the meal is kind to the mid-week budget, however "vin ordinaire" goes down well with the Mediterranean suppers.

SEAFOOD CASSEROLE
MOCHA GÂTEAU

For 6 servings

Seafood Casserole

    1 pound filleted white fish
        (haddock or whiting)
    4 ounces peeled shrimps
    2 hard boiled eggs
    2 ounces flour
    2 ounces butter
    1 pint milk
    6 rashers bacon
    4 tomatoes
    salt and pepper
    1 packet instant mashed potato

Place fish in a dish with half the milk, ½ ounce butter and the seasoning. Cover and cook for 20 minutes at 325°F or Gas Mark 3. Make a *roux* by melting the rest of the butter in a saucepan and adding flour. Cook without browning. Add the rest of the milk and stir to make a thick sauce, and then add the liquid from the fish. Season the flaked fish and chop up the hard boiled eggs. Place the fish, eggs and sauce in an ovenproof dish and cover with lightly grilled bacon rashers and sliced tomatoes. Make up instant mashed potato with an egg and pipe or fork on top of the casserole. Brush over with a little egg and cook in the oven for 20 minutes at 350°F or Gas Mark 4.

When you brew up the coffee afterwards serve this delicious gâteau.

Mocha Gâteau

    6 ounces margarine
    6 ounces caster sugar
    1 tablespoon cocoa *and*
    1 dessertspoon instant coffee,
        blended
    with 2 tablespoons warm water
    3 eggs
    6 ounces self-raising flour

Cream the fat to a light fluffy texture. Add the coffee and cocoa mixture and continue to cream. When it is well blended, add the eggs one by one with a tablespoon of self-raising flour with the last egg. Sieve in the remaining flour and fold in with a tablespoon. Bake in two 7-inch sandwich tins in a moderate oven, 350°F or Gas Mark 4, for 20 minutes.

ICING:
2 ounces margarine or butter
8 ounces icing sugar
1 tablespoon cocoa
1 dessertspoon instant coffee,
   blended with 2 tablespoons milk
24 walnuts

Cream the margarine with a little icing sugar until soft and fluffy. Add the cocoa and coffee mixture with the remaining icing sugar and mix thoroughly.
After the cake has cooled, spread icing in the middle and round the sides. Roll the sides of the cake in chopped walnuts. Spread remaining cream icing on top. Decorate with 6 walnuts.

Mediterranean Suppers

For 6 servings
Spaghetti Bolognese

1½ pounds spaghetti
2 ounces butter
freshly ground pepper
¼ teaspoon freshly ground nutmeg
bolognese sauce

Bolognese Sauce

2 tablespoons oil
1 ounce butter
1 large onion, finely chopped
1 clove garlic, crushed
1 carrot, finely chopped
1 stick celery, finely chopped
1 pound minced beef
2 tablespoons tomato purée
1 small can tomatoes (optional)
¼ teaspoon oregano
¼ pint red wine
½ pint beef stock

Sweat the vegetables in the butter and oil. Add the minced beef and cook until brown. Add remaining ingredients and simmer for 45 minutes. 2 tablespoons cream can be added just before serving.
Cook the spaghetti in a large saucepan of boiling water as directed on packet (some spaghetti takes longer to cook than others, usually 12-14 minutes for "al dente" spaghetti).

When cooked, drain in a collander. Melt butter in the saucepan and return the spaghetti. Add pepper and nutmeg and swirl around. Serve with Parmesan cheese.

Lasagne al Forno

This is a wide, flat ribbon of pasta which makes a delicious supper. It can easily be prepared beforehand.

For 6 servings
1¼ pounds lasagne
¾ pint Bolognese sauce (see previous recipe)
1 pint white sauce (see p. 17)
substitute 4 tablespoons of milk for same quantity of cream in the sauce
4 ounces grated Gruyère cheese

Cook the lasagne in a large saucepan of boiling salted water for 15 minutes. Drain. Butter an ovenproof dish and place a layer of lasagne on the bottom, then a layer of Bolognese sauce, then another layer of lasagne and then a layer of white sauce, seasoning each layer as you go. Repeat this process, pouring the remaining white sauce over the top and then add cheese. Cook in a moderate oven, 350°F or Gas Mark 4, until brown and bubbling, about 25 minutes. Make the sauces beforehand then all you need is a few minutes for preparation.

Pizza

This is a savoury flan with a bread base instead of pastry which can be prepared in advance and then reheated before serving.
For 2 persons.
Dough: see dinner roll recipe (p. 24) and use one-third of the quantities given.

FILLING:
1 tablespoon oil or 1 ounce butter
1 medium can tomatoes
1 medium onion, finely chopped
½ teaspoon oregano
salt and pepper

GARNISH:
2 ounces Parmesan cheese
12 black olives
1 small tin anchovies

Allow dough to rise as directed in the recipe.

Mediterranean Suppers

Then knead on a floured board. Flatten out into a swiss roll tin or a 10-inch Pyrex plate. Take a small piece of dough and roll into a long sausage shape. Dampen around the edge of the Pizza and place on the rolled dough. Heat the oil or butter in a skillet and cook the onion for a few minutes. Add the remaining ingredients for the filling. Garnish with halved olives and anchovy fillets. Brush the top with oil and cook in a hot oven, 425°F or Gas Mark 7, for about 15 minutes.

You can experiment with your own favourite tomato filling or use a Bolognese sauce as an alternative.

Aubergines
Make sure the skins are firm and shiny. They are delicious stuffed with meat mixtures. Aubergines are sometimes called egg-plants.

Ratatouille

8 tablespoons oil
2 large onions
1 pound tomatoes
1 pound courgettes
1 pound aubergines
1 red pepper
1 green pepper
2 cloves garlic, crushed
1 bay leaf
$\frac{1}{4}$ teaspoon rosemary
$\frac{1}{4}$ teaspoon basil
salt and pepper

Slice courgettes and aubergines, sprinkle with salt and lemon juice and allow to stand for 15 minutes. Cut onions into rings and sweat in oil. Add sliced tomatoes, courgettes, aubergines, sliced and deseeded peppers, garlic and herbs.

Red and Green Peppers

Cover with a lid and bring to the boil. Remove lid and simmer until all the liquid has evaporated —be careful not to overdo this otherwise it will burn.

Quiche Lorraine

PASTRY:
8 ounces plain flour
4 ounces butter or margarine
1 ounce grated cheese
½ teaspoon salt
1 egg yolk
2 tablespoons water

FILLING:
4 ounces lean bacon
3 eggs
¼ pint thick cream
1 ounce butter
salt and pepper

Rub fat into flour and salt. Mix with egg and water. Allow the pastry to rest for a while in the refrigerator. Roll out and line a flan ring or pie plate. Prick the bottom with a fork. Cut the bacon into small slices and boil for 5 minutes. Drain. Mix eggs, cream, salt and pepper. Dot uncooked pastry with butter. Put the bacon into the flan case and pour on egg mixture. Bake in a hot oven, 400°F or Gas Mark 6 until egg is set.

Round off any of these savoury dishes with fresh fruit or on the following spectacular note.

Flaming Pears
Try this sweet. It really is different.

Flaming Pears

2 large cans halved pears
3 ounces creamed cheese
1 tablespoon sugar
1 ounce chopped walnuts
6 tablespoons water
1 tablespoon cornflour
10 ounces raspberries (frozen or canned)
4 tablespoons brandy

Filling:
Mix cream cheese, sugar with enough pear syrup to achieve a spreading consistency. Stir in the walnuts. Spread the mixture on the flat surface of the pear halves, using about 1 tablespoon for each. Press two halves together, making up six whole pears.

Sauce:
Blend water and cornflour and stir in raspberries. Cook and stir until thick. Sieve and serve warm.
Warm brandy in a ladle, pour over pears and ignite. Pour the sauce on the pears.

Television Supper

Sometimes a special film or programme on "the box" merits a meal on a tray shared with friends. Should the programme prove disappointing, the following meal should lift you from your twilight gloom.

For 4 servings

CELERY SOUP
BACON & EGG PIE
  TOMATO SAUCE

Celery Soup

Celery Soup

  1 large onion, finely chopped
  1 head celery, chopped in small pieces
  ½ teaspoon lovage
  2 pints stock (use a stock cube)
  ½ pint milk
  1½ ounces butter
  1 tablespoon flour or cornflour
  salt and pepper

Melt one ounce of the butter and sweat onion and celery. Add stock, seasoning and lovage. Bring to the boil and simmer for 1 hour. Sieve or liquidise. Melt remaining butter, add flour, stir in milk and the sieved soup. Adjust seasoning and add a little chopped, cooked celery as a garnish with 1 dessertspoonful of cream, if desired.

Bacon & Egg Pie

  6 ounces short crust pastry (see p. 43)
  4-6 rashers bacon
  4 small tomatoes
  4 mushrooms, cut into slices
  4 eggs
  salt and pepper
  Worcester sauce

Roll out two-thirds of the pastry for an 8-inch flan ring. Line the bottom of the ring with pastry, do not trim. Gently fry the bacon and mushrooms for a few minutes then allow to cool. Line the bottom of the pastry with bacon and mushrooms. Break eggs into flan whole, season and cover with sliced, skinned tomatoes and season again. Roll out remaining pastry, damp the bottom edge of the ring and cover. Seal the edge of the flan with a rolling pin. Slit the top or make a hole in the centre and decorate with pastry shapes. Brush out the egg shells and use to glaze the top of the pastry. Cook for 25 minutes at 400°F or Gas Mark 6, on the second top oven shelf.

Tomato Sauce

  1 tablespoon olive oil
  1½ pounds ripe tomatoes
    (or 1 large can)
  1 teaspoon sugar
  2 ounces onion, sliced
  1 stalk celery, sliced
  bouquet garni **(sprig of parsley,**
    bay leaf and basil)
  salt and pepper
  ½ teaspoon tomato purée
  few drops of Worcester sauce

Heat the oil and sweat onion and celery. Add the tomatoes cut into quarters. Add herbs, seasoning, Worcester sauce, purée and simmer for 30 minutes. Sieve and reduce if necessary.

CREOLE STUFFED PEPPERS
CRUNCHY APPLE FLAN

Creole Stuffed Peppers

6 peppers
1 ounce butter
8 ounces cooked Patna rice
1 large onion, finely chopped
8 ounces minced beef
½ teaspoon chilli powder
1 tablespoon tomato purée
3 tablespoons water

Blanch the peppers in boiling salted water for 5 minutes. Melt the butter, sauté the onion, add the meat and brown. Add chilli powder, the tops of the peppers finely chopped, water, tomato purée and simmer for 20 minutes. Mix with the rice. Stuff the mixture into de-seeded peppers. Paint the peppers with oil and cook in a moderate oven, 350°F or Gas Mark 4, for 30 minutes.

Crunchy Apple Flan

4 ounces Corn Flakes
3 ounces butter or margarine
2 tablespoons syrup

Crush the cornflakes and pour on melted fat. Use to line a pie plate or flan ring. Chill in the refrigerator. Fill with sliced apples which have been stewed in water and sugar, flavoured with cloves. Decorate with cream.

Cold Weather Suppers

WATERCRESS SOUP
MACARONI BAKE

Watercress Soup

8 ounces watercress
½ ounce butter
1 pint stock
salt and pepper
1 tablespoon cornflour
¼ pint milk
2 tablespoons thin cream

Wash the watercress and remove coarse stalks. Melt the butter in a saucepan, add watercress, reserving a little for a garnish. Toss over a gentle heat for 3 minutes. Add stock, seasoning, cover and simmer gently for 15 minutes. Sieve then add blended cornflour and milk. Bring to the boil, stir and cook for 5 minutes. Adjust the seasoning.

Macaroni Bake

1 pound elbow macaroni
1 ounce butter
1 onion, finely chopped
8 ounces bacon
8 ounces tomatoes
1 red or green pepper
4 ounces mushrooms
1½ ounces butter
1½ ounces flour
1 pint milk
salt and pepper
4 ounces cheese, grated

Cook the macaroni in boiling, salted water for 7 minutes. Drain. Grill the bacon for 2-3 minutes; slice pepper and mushrooms and sauté in 1 ounce butter for a few minutes. Make a white sauce with flour, butter and milk as on p. 17. Mix macaroni with seasoning,

Creole Stuffed Peppers

3 ounces cheese, vegetables and white sauce. Spread a layer in a buttered casserole, cover with slices of bacon and then with slices of uncooked tomato. Cover with half of remaining macaroni mixture then add further bacon and tomato. Use the remaining macaroni mixture and tomato slices as a topping and sprinkle with grated cheese. Bake in a moderate oven, 350°F or Gas Mark 4, for 25 minutes. Serve fresh fruit if another course is required or:

Pineapple Upside Down Cake

    4 ounces margarine
    4 ounces caster sugar
    2 eggs
    4 ounces self-raising flour
    5 pineapple rings
    5 cherries
    2 tablespoons brown sugar
    ½ ounce butter

Cream fat and sugar until light and fluffy. Beat in eggs one at a time, sieve flour and fold in with a tablespoon. Grease an 8-inch sandwich tin and spread melted butter and brown sugar on the bottom. Place rings of pineapple on the bottom of the tin then cover with mixture. Cook in a warm oven, 325°F or Gas Mark 3 for 40 minutes. Allow to cool slightly and turn upside down out of tin. Decorate centre of the pineapple rings with a cherry and serve with cream.

Turning out the Pineapple Upside Down Cake

**KIDNEY SOUP WITH DUMPLINGS
FLUFFY OMELETTE**

Kidney Soup with Dumplings

    1 ounce butter
    8 ounces kidney
    1 onion, finely chopped
    1 carrot, chopped
    2 sticks celery, chopped
    1½ pints stock
    1 tablespoon tomato purée
    salt and pepper
    ½ teaspoon thyme
    1 ounce cornflour
    4 tablespoons milk

Melt the butter in a saucepan and sauté the vegetables and chopped kidney. Add stock, tomato purée and seasoning. Bring to the boil and simmer for about 2 hours. Sieve. Add blended cornflour and milk. Simmer for 30 minutes with dumplings or until dumplings are cooked.

Dumplings

    4 ounces self-raising flour
    2 ounces shredded suet
    ½ onion, finely chopped or grated
    ½ teaspoon mixed herbs
    salt and pepper

Sieve the flour into a bowl and mix with the other ingredients. Mix with enough water to make a dough. Roll into about 16 balls and cook in the soup as directed.

Fluffy Omelette

    2 eggs, separated
    2 teaspoons caster sugar
    1 ounce butter
    2 tablespoons red jam

This makes 1 omelette to serve two.
Whisk egg whites until light and fluffy. Whisk egg yolk and sugar until light and fluffy. Heat the oven to 350°F or Gas Mark 4. Heat the butter in an omelette pan until it bubbles. Then fold in the egg yolk mixture to the egg white mixture and pour into the pan. Allow to cook over a gentle heat for 2-3 minutes. Then put into the oven for about 10 minutes. Alternatively, it can be finished off under the grill. Sprinkle with caster sugar and spread with warmed jam.

Macaroni Bake

Savoury Supper

If you want to make all your chicken portions equal, it is possible to buy packets of drumsticks or breasts in the supermarkets.

Boiled Rice
Paprika Chicken

PAPRIKA CHICKEN
   RICE
      BAKED BANANAS
FRUIT TRANCHE

For 4 servings

Paprika Chicken

1 (3 pound) roasting chicken
2 tablespoons oil
1 large onion, finely chopped
1 green pepper
2 tomatoes
2 teaspoons flour
salt
2 teaspoons paprika
¼ pint stock or water
2 tablespoons thick cream

Wash the chicken then rub with a piece of lemon. Joint into 6 pieces. Heat oil and fry onion until slightly golden then add chopped pepper and quartered tomatoes. Toss chicken pieces in a polythene bag with flour. Brown the chicken on all sides. Sprinkle with salt and paprika, add the fried onions, pepper and tomatoes, and the stock or water. Bring to the boil then simmer for about 30 minutes until chicken is tender. Alternatively, cook for 40 minutes in a moderate oven, 350°F or Gas Mark 4. Stir in cream just before serving. This dish can be prepared well in advance. Then before serving, reheat the chicken on a serving dish covered with foil, reheat the sauce then stir in the cream and pour over the chicken.

Rice

1 pound long grain rice
1¾ pints water
2 level teaspoons salt
1 teaspoon oil

Wash rice in cold water and cook in boiling, salted water with the oil added. Allow to come to the boil again and boil for 8-10 minutes, stirring occasionally. When rice is cooked, strain in a large sieve and run under hot water until all the starch is rinsed out. Melt some butter or margarine in a saucepan and return rinsed rice. Cover with a lid and steam dry before serving.

Baked Bananas

4 bananas, peeled
1 ounce butter
¼ teaspoon paprika

Melt the butter and paint over the bananas. Sprinkle with paprika. Bake in a moderate oven, 350°F or Gas Mark 4, for 15 minutes.

Alternative method:
This is from the Carribean. Simply put the unskinned bananas in a moderate oven, 350°F or Gas Mark 4, for 25 minutes. Allow to cool slightly, remove skins and serve.

Flaky Pastry

8 ounces plain flour
6 ounces cooking fat (or cooking fat and margarine mixed)
squeeze of lemon juice
½ level teaspoon salt
cold water to mix

Sieve the flour and salt into a basin. Divide fat into four. Rub a quarter into the flour. Make a pliable dough with lemon juice and cold water. Knead lightly with the finger-tips to an even texture. Roll into an oblong of about ¼-inch thick. Put the second quarter of fat in small

knobs evenly over two thirds of the dough. Fold into three so that the layers of dough and fat alternate. Turn dough once to the left so that the fold is to the left hand. Roll out again into an oblong. Repeat the process twice until all the fat is used. Fold into three again. Seal edges. Leave in a cool place for at least 1 hour.

The pastry is improved if it is left to rest for 15 minutes or so in a cool place between each rolling. It is a good plan to make the pastry the day before it is required.

Fruit Tranche

flaky pastry (half the quantity of previous recipe)
1 medium size can cherries
2 tablespoons sieved apricot jam
¼ pint of fruit syrup from the can
2 teaspoons cornflour
1 dessertspoon water
1 egg, beaten

Make the pastry. Roll out to a rectangle 10 inches by 6 inches. Cut a 1-inch strip from each of the 4 sides. Put the rectangle of pastry on a damp baking sheet and prick all over with a fork; brush the edges with beaten egg or milk. Position the pastry strips carefully on the edges of the rectangle, pressing gently to bond without flattening the pastry. Allow to rest in a cool place for 15-20 minutes. Brush the top of the pastry strip with beaten egg or milk. Bake at the top of the oven for 20 minutes at 425°F or Gas Mark 7. Cool on a wire tray. Drain the fruit and arrange in the cooled pastry case. Warm the apricot jam and brush over the top edge of the pastry case. Put the fruit syrup on to boil. Blend the cornflour with the water. Pour the boiling syrup on to the blended cornflour, stirring continuously. Return the mixture to the saucepan, bring to the boil and cook until it becomes clear; spoon over the fruit.

Brush over the Bananas with melted butter

Noodle Supper

QUICK TOMATO SOUP
NOODLE PORK SUPPER
SAMANTHA'S SALAD
APRICOT FLAN

For 6 servings

Quick Tomato Soup

$\frac{3}{4}$ pint tomato juice
$\frac{3}{4}$ pint stock (made from chicken cube)
1 onion, sliced
1 stick celery, chopped
6 peppercorns
$\frac{1}{2}$ teaspoon sugar
1 tablespoon lemon juice
salt and pepper

Leaving out the lemon juice, heat the rest of the ingredients together in a saucepan and simmer for 15 minutes. Strain, add lemon juice and serve hot or cold with a slice of lemon.

Noodle Pork Supper

12 ounces of pork, minced,
or sausage meat
1 egg
salt and pepper
$\frac{1}{4}$ teaspoon sage and thyme, mixed

NOODLE MIXTURE:
1 pound noodles
1 pint cheese sauce:
2 ounces butter
2 ounces flour
1 pint milk
4 ounces cheese
½ teaspoon mustard
pinch of cayenne
½ green pepper
½ red pepper
1 apple, diced

Mix minced pork with egg, seasoning and herbs. Form into 6 rounds and fry in oil until both sides are cooked. Keep warm. Sauté peppers and apples. Cook noodles in boiling, salted water for about 7 minutes. Drain then toss in butter with freshly grated nutmeg. To make the cheese sauce, make the white sauce as on p. 17 and then add the cheese. Mix the noodles, cheese sauce and peppers, arrange pork rounds on top and heat in a warm oven before serving.

Samantha's Salad

1 lettuce
1 apple
1 orange
3 eggs, hard boiled
6 walnuts
6 radishes
juice of 2 lemons

Arrange lettuce round the salad bowl. Chop apple, orange, walnuts and radishes, then toss in lemon juice. Cut eggs in wedges and arrange salad.

Apricot Flan

6 ounces rich shortcrust pastry
  (see p. 9)
1 large can apricots
2 teaspoons arrowroot
2 ounces white breadcrumbs
½ ounce brown sugar
½ ounce butter

Bake a flan case blind and allow to cool. Put breadcrumbs and brown sugar in a Swiss roll tin, dotted with butter. Place in a moderate oven, 350°F or Gas Mark 4, turning occasionally until crumbs are golden brown. Allow to cool. Drain the apricots and thicken the juice with arrowroot. Arrange apricots in the flan case, pour over the thickened juice and sprinkle with the breadcrumbs.

Apricot Flan
Try this delicious crispy crumb topping for a flan with a difference.

Alternatively, fill a flan case with cherries, peaches or gooseberries or grapes and decorate with cooked pastry shapes.

CHAPTER 4

Occasional Parties
Guy Fawkes

Cold weather and vigorous activity can be guaranteed to set appetites rocketing on Bonfire Night. And there are usually many mouths to feed. It's quite amazing how many uncles and aunts your children suddenly acquire when you announce that you're having a Guy Fawkes' party! So make sure that after the fireworks the food helps the party to go with a bang. Here are some sizzling recipes to stoke up the revellers and keep the party glowing.

BANGERS AND BACON
BEANS AND BURGERS
DOUBLE DECKER SANDWICHES
ROCKET CAKE
GUY'S HOT CHOCOLATE
VANILLA TABLET

Bangers and Bacon

8 large fat sausages
8 bacon rashers

Grill the sausages until cooked. Roll the bacon rashers round them and cook in a moderate oven, 350°F or Gas Mark 4, until bacon is cooked.

Beans and Burgers

10 ounces minced beef
$\frac{1}{4}$ teaspoon oregano
salt and pepper
1 giant can of beans
1 packet instant mashed potatoes

Mix beef, oregano and seasoning together. Make 8 patties of the beef and cook in a frying pan with a little oil until brown and cooked. Heat beans in the bottom of a casserole. Make up instant mashed potatoes as directed, adding an egg, cheese and seasoning. Put burgers on top of the beans then pipe or fork on cheese potato mixture. Garnish each burger with a wedge of tomato. Warm through in a moderate oven, 350°F or Gas Mark 4.

Double Decker Sandwiches

8 slices of bread buttered on 1 side
8 slices of bread buttered on both sides
4 slices ham
1 lettuce, shredded
4 tomatoes, sliced
4 slices cheese
salt and pepper
mustard

Cut the crusts from the bread. Arrange lettuce and sliced tomato on 4 slices of the bread buttered on one side. Sandwich with slices of bread buttered on both sides. Place on a layer of cheese and then another piece of double-buttered bread. Place on a layer of lettuce and ham with mustard, and then finish off with remaining bread buttered on one side. Cut double decker in two, making eight sandwiches.

Vanilla Tablet

1 pound sugar
1 can condensed milk
2 ounces butter
2 tablespoons water, $\frac{1}{4}$ pint milk
1 teaspoon vanilla

Put all the ingredients into a thick-bottomed saucepan, over a low heat. Stir until all the sugar is dissolved and bring to the boil. Boil steadily until a drop of the mixture forms a soft ball when placed in water. Have a buttered swiss roll tin ready. Remove the mixture from the heat and stand the saucepan in cold water. Beat until thick. Pour into the tin. When almost set cut into small pieces.

Rocket Cake

- **2 large eggs**
- **2½ ounces caster sugar**
- **2½ ounces plain flour**

Line a swiss roll tin with grease-proof paper. Preheat the oven to 425°F or Gas Mark 7. Sieve the flour and set aside. Whisk the eggs and sugar together until light and thick in a mixing bowl over a pan of warm water. After taking the bowl from the heat, continue beating for a further 2 minutes. Sieve the flour over the mixture and gently fold in with a metal spoon. Pour into prepared tin and spread evenly. Cook on the second shelf from the top of the oven for 7-8 minutes until golden brown.
Fudge icing to decorate: melt 2 ounces margarine and 3 dessertspoons orange juice in a saucepan. Remove from the heat and sieve in 8 ounces icing sugar. Beat well until cool.

Stand the swiss roll on end on a plate or cooking board. Cover with fudge icing and mark with a fork. Make a cone of coloured paper for the rocket, using a 6-inch diameter circle. Make fins with milk flake. You can make a face on the rocket, using sweets for eyes, ears and nose.

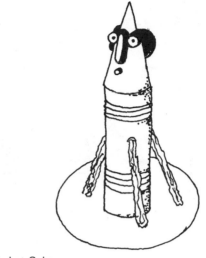

Rocket Cake

Hallowe'en

Hallowe'en is a day which is made much more of in Scotland than south of the border, with the children dressing themselves up to go out 'guising'. However, children in all countries welcome any excuse for a party and Hallowe'en parties can be such fun. Different regions have traditional Hallowe'en dishes.

HALLOWE'EN TEAS
SANDWICHES
GINGER WITCHES AND CATS
HALLOWE'EN APPLES
HOT BLACKCURRANT JUICE

Sandwich Fillings

Tuna Fish

- **1 ounce butter**
- **1 small can tuna fish**
- **2 tablespoons tomato ketchup**
- **salt and pepper**

Ginger Witches   Ginger Cats
Decorate with liquorice and sweets

Banana

- **1 ounce butter**
- **2 mashed bananas**
- **½ teaspoon cinnamon**
- **1 tablespoon lemon juice**
- **1 teaspoon brown sugar**

Peanut Butter

$\frac{1}{2}$ ounce butter
2 tablespoons peanut butter

Egg and Cheese

1 ounce butter
2 portions cream cheese
salt and pepper
1 egg, hard-boiled and sieved

Cheese Parsley Butter

4 ounces cream cheese
pinch of cayenne
2 ounces butter
1 teaspoon parsley

I find that the easiest way of making sandwiches is to cream the butter and mix it with the sandwich spread ingredients. This saves spreading the bread twice. Make sure that the bread is completely covered with filling as nothing is more irritating than a sandwich with nothing round the edges. This was my pet hate when I was a child!
It is also a good idea to put marker flags on the plates with different kinds of sandwiches just in case some children have dislikes.

Here you see apples made into witches and cats.

Ginger Witches and Cats

6 ounces plain flour
1 teaspoon cinnamon
2 teaspoons ground ginger
3 ounces soft brown sugar
3 ounces margarine
1 rounded tablespoon golden syrup
$\frac{1}{2}$ tablespoon treacle
$\frac{1}{4}$ teaspoon bicarbonate of soda,
    dissolved in 1 tablespoon milk

Sieve flour and spice in a bowl and stir in sugar. Melt margarine, syrup and treacle in a saucepan over a low heat. Cool then pour over dry ingredients and mix well. Stir in the bicarbonate of soda and milk. Shape into small round balls and place well apart on a greased baking sheet. Bake in a moderate oven, 350°F or Gas Mark 4, for 25 minutes on the second shelf from the top. Allow to cool on a wire tray.

ICING:
2 ounces margarine or butter
6 ounces icing sugar, sieved
1 tablespoon milk
a few drops of pink colouring

Spread icing on ginger biscuits and use small

sweets and liquorice to make witches and cat's faces.

Hallowe'en Apples

8 apples

TOFFEE:
8 ounces sugar
3 tablespoons water
1 teaspoon vinegar
Popcorn or rice crispies

Make the toffee by dissolving sugar slowly in water and then boil rapidly until toffee is slightly thick but still clear . . . the stage before it would be used for toffee apples. Dip the apples in the toffee and then in the popcorn or rice crispies. Sit them in paper cups and decorate faces with sweets, liquorice and paper hats.

Blackcurrant Juice

½ bottle blackcurrant juice
juice of 2 lemons

Divide amongst mugs and pour hot water on before serving.

Try a favourite Scottish Hallowe'en party game called 'Ducking for apples'. You need a large bowl, half-filled with water, on which you float lots of small apples. Stir the water round and make the children take turns to lean over the back of a chair with a fork in their mouth. The idea is to spear one of the swirling apples. The one who spears the most apples out of 6 efforts is the winner. Make sure they don't start spearing while you are stirring—they might well spear you!

Easter

Hot Cross Buns

1 pound plain flour
1 teaspoon mixed spice
½ teaspoon salt
2 ounces margarine
6 ounces currants
½ ounce chopped peel
2 ounces caster sugar
½ ounce dried yeast (1 ounce fresh)
12 tablespoons milk
1 egg

CROSSES:
2 ounces shortcrust pastry (see p. 9)

GLAZE:
2 tablespoons milk
2 tablespoons water
2 tablespoons sugar

Hot Cross Buns

Warm a mixing bowl and sieve in flour and spice. Rub in the margarine until the consistency is of fine breadcrumbs. Add fruit and sugar, reserving 1 teaspoon caster sugar for the yeast. Cream together the yeast and sugar then add warmed milk; alternatively, make up dried yeast as directed on packet. Add the egg to the yeast and milk, mix the dough with your hand until it is fairly soft. Turn out on to a floured board and knead for a few minutes. Return to the bowl and cover with a cloth or polythene sheet. Allow to double in size: this will take over an hour in a warm place (see notes on yeast cookery, p. 24). Turn out the risen dough, knead lightly and divide into 12 equal balls. Shape into buns and allow to rise on a greased baking sheet for about 25 minutes. Cover with cloth or polythene. Make crosses, brush the top of the buns with a little milk and place a cross on each. Bake for 15-20 minutes in a hot oven, 425°F or Gas Mark 7. Boil the glaze for a few minutes and brush on while the buns are still hot.

Simnel Cake

6 ounces butter or margarine
6 ounces caster sugar
4 eggs
8 ounces plain flour
½ teaspoon salt
1 teaspoon baking powder
1 teaspoon mixed spice
1 teaspoon cinnamon
12 ounces mixed fruit, washed
2 ounces candied peel, chopped
juice and rind of lemon

ALMOND PASTE:
8 ounces ground almonds
6 ounces caster sugar
4 ounces icing sugar, sieved
2 egg yolks
juice of 1 lemon

Easter Chickens, for decoration

Make up almond paste first. Mix the sugar and ground almonds together. Make a well in the centre and add egg yolks and lemon juice. Mix with a small palette knife or fork and knead to a smooth paste. Roll one-third of the paste into a round which is slightly smaller than a prepared 8-inch tin. Put remaining paste in the refrigerator wrapped up. Remember to take it out to stand for a while at room temperature before using.

Cream sugar and fat until light and fluffy. Sieve flour, salt and spices together. Beat in the eggs, one at a time, using a little of the sieved flour with the last two eggs. Fold in remaining sieved flour, fruit and lemon juice. Turn half the cake mixture into the greased tin and then the round of almond paste which is smaller than the cake tin. Tap the tin to level out mixture and then add the remaining cake mixture. Level out and hollow slightly in the middle. Put the cake in the centre of a moderate oven, 350°F or Gas Mark 4, for 40 minutes; lower heat to 325°F or Gas Mark 3, and bake for a further 2 hours. Allow to cool.

To finish cake: divide the remaining paste into two. If the top of the cake is not absolutely level, patch it with a little almond paste. Roll out one piece of the paste to the size of the top of the cake. Use caster sugar for rolling out. Brush the top of the cake with hot, sieved apricot jam and turn on to the paste. Turn upright and pinch up the edge of the marzipan.

Roll the remaining paste into the shape of eggs; glaze these and the cake with egg and brown under the grill.

Arrange the egg shapes with chickens on top of the cake and tie a yellow satin ribbon round the middle.

Easter Biscuits

For 12-14 biscuits
4 ounces butter or margarine
4 ounces caster sugar
1 egg
8 ounces plain flour
pinch of salt
½ teaspoon ground cinnamon
½ teaspoon mixed spice
grated rind of 1 lemon
2 ounces currants
1 tablespoon milk

Cream fat and sugar until light and fluffy, then add egg and milk. Sieve flour and spices and add, together with the lemon rind and fruit, to the creamed mixture. Mix to a stiff consistency and roll out ¼-inch thick. Cut with a 4-inch cutter into rounds. Brush with egg white. Bake in a moderate oven, 350°F or Gas Mark 4, until golden brown. Dredge with caster sugar.

It is always as well to keep something in store over the Easter holiday in case you have visitors dropping in out of the blue. In any event it is a good idea to have something prepared before the holiday so that you can have a holiday as well. The following pie and cakes are convenient and delicious. If the weather permits the pie makes an ideal picnic meal.

Veal and Ham Pie

HOT WATER CRUST PASTRY:
1 pound flour
6 ounces lard
1 teaspoon salt
$\frac{1}{4}$ pint milk or water

FILLING:
$1\frac{1}{2}$ pounds lean veal
$\frac{1}{2}$ pound gammon
pinch of pepper
1 teaspoon salt
grated rind of $\frac{1}{2}$ lemon
1 tablespoon parsley, chopped
1 hard-boiled egg
$\frac{1}{4}$ pint stock
1 dessertspoon gelatine
beaten egg
milk

Add the lard to the milk or water and bring to the boil in a small saucepan. Then add the flour sieved with the salt. Use a wooden spoon to beat into a stiff mixture. Knead well on a wooden board and keep warm.

Cut the veal and ham into small pieces, making sure to remove any pieces of fat. Mix with the seasoning, lemon rind and parsley.

Thoroughly lard a raised pie mould or mould the pastry in a cake tin and put it on a greased baking tray.

Set aside part of the pastry for the lid and roll out the rest to a $\frac{1}{2}$-inch thickness. Line the bottom of the mould with the pastry and knead well with the knuckles from the centre to the edges to remove any air. Line the sides of the tin, pressing the pastry well in with the thumbs. See that the pastry overlaps the top of the rim. Take half of the filling and pack in well. Place the egg in the middle then cover with the rest of the filling. Roll out a pastry lid and place it on top after damping the edges of the pie. Press the edges firmly and trim. Make a small hole in the centre of the top, brush with beaten egg and milk, and arrange small leaves of pastry on top as a decoration.

Cook in the centre of a hot oven, 400°F or Gas Mark 6, for 20 minutes and then 355°F, or Gas Mark 4 for a further $2\frac{1}{2}$ hours. Make the pastry a shiny brown by occasional brushing with beaten egg and milk during baking. After the pie has been in for $1\frac{1}{2}$ hours, remove the mould, brush again with egg and milk, and put back in the oven.

After the pie has cooled, pour jellied stock through the hole.

Gingerbread

8 ounces plain flour
4 ounces butter
8 ounces black treacle
$\frac{1}{4}$ pint milk
2 eggs
2 ounces sugar
1 teaspoon mixed spice
2 teaspoons ground ginger
$\frac{1}{2}$ teaspoon bicarbonate soda
2 ounces sultanas
1 ounce glacé cherries (halved)
1 ounce crystallised ginger (chopped)

Grease a square 7-inch cake tin and line it with greaseproof paper. Warm the butter, treacle, sugar and milk all together in a large saucepan. Allow to cool. Blend in the beaten eggs. Add the cooled mixture to the sieved dry ingredients. Add the fruit. Turn the mixture into the prepared tin. Bake slightly below the middle of a slow oven 325°F or Gas Mark 3 for about $1\frac{1}{4}$ hours.

Banana Cake

10 ounces self-raising flour
4 ounces butter or margarine
6 ounces brown sugar
3 eggs
2 bananas
1 level teaspoon cinnamon
4 tablespoons milk

Cream together the butter and sugar until soft and fluffy. Mash the bananas with a fork and beat into the creamed mixture. Add the eggs one by one with, if necessary, a little sieved flour. Add milk. Fold in the sieved flour and cinnamon. Bake in a moderate oven 325°F or Gas Mark 3, for $1\frac{1}{2}$ hours.

This cake is delicious as a sweet with bananas and cream, or as a special tea-time treat, it can be sandwiched with chocolate butter icing.

CHAPTER 5

Recipes for Tea Parties

It seems strange that although there is now a great vogue for Victoriana, no one has really got round to reviving one of the glories of that age—the Tea Party. This is the ideal way of entertaining friends who find it difficult to get out in the evening because of finding someone to look after the children.

Even if you are busy during the week, it is not too difficult to find time at the occasional week-end to do some baking.

There is something very satisfying—if old-fashioned—in providing a well laid tea table. Moreover, it seems to bring out the very best in your friend's children.

Instead of filling them up on sandwiches, try them instead on continental pancakes—the *pannakoekes* of Holland and the *crêpes* of France—with sweet or savoury fillings.

Crêpe Batter

> **8 ounces flour**
> **½ teaspoon salt**
> **3 eggs**
> **¾ pint milk**
> **7 tablespoons oil**

Make the batter several hours before using. Sieve the flour and salt into a bowl, make a well in the centre and put in the eggs. Beat hard with a wooden spoon and add the milk gradually, beating constantly until you have a smooth batter. Finally add the oil.

For making crêpes use a pan which is set aside solely for this purpose. The crêpes will stick on a washed pan so wipe with a paper towel after use. Stir batter well before using. Then pour 1½ tablespoons into a hot pan and tilt it until the mixture forms a thin layer. Turn up the heat for a few seconds and then lower it. Turn with a wide spatula and cook for one minute on the other side. Store the crêpes one on top of the other in a warm oven or between two plates over warm water.

Fillings for Crêpes

1) CHICKEN:
> **½ pint white sauce (see p. 17)**
> **8 ounces chopped cooked chicken**
> **salt and pepper**

Mix ingredients together, fill crêpes and roll.

2) BACON:
> **4 tablespoons oil**
> **6 rashers bacon, diced**
> **2 large onions, diced**
> **paprika**
> **salt and pepper**
> **2 tablespoons tomato ketchup**

Sauté onion and bacon till cooked. Add the other ingredients. Spread on crêpes and fold.

Now for baking your own bread. If you are unfamiliar with yeast cookery, see the notes on p. 24.

Wholemeal Bread

> **3 pounds wholemeal flour**
> **1 ounce fat**
> **5 teaspoons salt**
> **1½ ounces yeast (or ¾ ounce dried yeast)**
> **1 teaspoon sugar**
> **1½ pints lukewarm water**

Sieve flour and salt into a warmed basin and leave in a warm place. Cream yeast and sugar in a basin and add ½ pint of the warmed water. If you use dried yeast, reconstitute as directed. Put the yeast mixture in a well made in the centre of the flour. Lightly dust with flour. Leave for about 15 minutes until the sponge breaks through. Cover with a clean cloth or polythene sheet. Then add melted fat and gradually work in the remaining water until you have a dough. Knead well and allow to rise in a warm place for about 45 minutes until it has doubled in size. Divide into three. Knead and shape into rolls. Place each roll in a lightly greased 2-pound loaf tin or divide dough into 6 rolls and place in 1-pound loaf tins or on greased baking sheets. Prove for at least 30 minutes in a warm place then bake in a hot oven, 450°F or Gas Mark 8. For Malt Bread, add 2 ounces warmed malt with the liquid to the flour.

Submarine Loaf

Cut a French loaf lengthwise into three and butter each length.

Fill the bottom layer with lettuce and sliced tomatoes; the next layer with canned salmon, seasoned with a little vinegar and salt and vinegar; the top layer with lettuce and cucumber. Top with the crustry parts of the loaf, stuck with sandwich flags or cocktail sticks with sliced gherkins. Cut and serve with knives and forks.

Tea Ring

6 ounces plain flour
$\frac{1}{4}$ teaspoon salt
$\frac{1}{2}$ ounce sugar
scant $\frac{1}{2}$ ounce fresh yeast
(or 1 teaspoon dried yeast)
scant $\frac{1}{4}$ pint warm milk
$\frac{1}{2}$ egg
FILLING:
1 ounce caster sugar
1 ounce ground almonds
Hot water to mix
ICING:
3 ounces icing sugar, sieved
warm water

Mix flour and salt, add most of the sugar. Cream the yeast with 1 teaspoon sugar, add warm milk and egg then mix to a dough. Knead lightly then allow to rise in a warm place until it doubles in size. Roll out in an oblong, spread on filling, damp edges and roll up. Form into a ring and prove on a greased baking sheet for 15 minutes. Bake in a hot oven, 425°F or Gas Mark 7, for 10 minutes. Reduce heat to 375°F or Gas Mark 5 and bake until golden brown. Spread with icing and sprinkle with chopped almonds.

Sultana Scones

8 ounces self-raising flour
1 teaspoon baking powder (optional)
2 ounces margarine
1 ounce caster sugar
2 ounces sultanas
scant $\frac{1}{4}$ pint milk

Sieve the flour and baking powder in a mixing bowl. Rub fat into the flour until the mixture has the texture of fine breadcrumbs. Knead mixture very lightly on a floured board and roll out to a $\frac{1}{2}$-inch thickness. Leave, if possible, on a greased baking sheet for at least 20 minutes before baking in a hot oven, 425°F or Gas Mark 7, for 10-12 minutes on the second top shelf. Serve hot with lots of butter.

Rock Buns

1 pound plain flour
$\frac{1}{4}$ teaspoon salt
6 ounces margarine
6 ounces caster sugar
4 ounces currants
2 ounces mixed peel
3 teaspoons baking powder
2 eggs
generous $\frac{1}{4}$ pint milk

Sieve flour and salt into a bowl. Cut the fat into the flour with a round ended knife then rub with finger tips until fine. Add sugar, fruit and baking powder. Mix with milk and egg to a stiff consistency. Cook in patty tins or in little heaps on a greased baking sheet in a hot oven, 425°F or Gas Mark 7, for 10-15 minutes.

Scotch Pancakes (Drop Scones)

8 ounces self-raising flour
2 teaspoons baking powder
pinch of salt
1 ounce caster sugar
1 egg
generous $\frac{1}{4}$ pint milk

Sieve the flour, baking powder and salt into a bowl. Stir in the sugar, egg and some of the milk. Beat the batter until bubbles appear on the surface. Add the remaining milk and allow batter to stand at least $\frac{1}{2}$ hour.

Stir once before using then preheat a girdle or strong frying pan on a moderate heat. Allow to heat up slowly. Grease with a piece of dripping wrapped in muslin or greaseproof paper. Drop 3 or 4 dessertspoons of the mixture on to the girdle or pan. Turn with a palette knife when bubbles appear on the surface. Cool on a wire tray and cover with a clean tea towel.

Serve with butter and jam. Any left over scones are delicious fried with bacon and eggs.

Truffle Cakes

6 ounces stale sponge cake
2 dessertspoons jam, warmed
1 teaspoon lemon juice
1 teaspoon almond essence
8 glacé cherries
4 ounces chocolate vermicelli

Mix sponge cake with jam, lemon juice and essence. Mould round the glacé cherries and roll in chocolate vermicelli. Leave in the refrigerator to firm.

Apricot Tarts

6 ounces short crust pastry (see p. 9)

CREAM FILLING:
1 ounce plain flour
2 ounces caster sugar
2 egg yolks
¼ pint milk
¼ pint apricot juice
1 small can apricot halves

GLAZE:
4 tablespoons apricot jam
1 tablespoon water

Make up the pastry and line the bottom of 12 patty tins. Prick the bottoms well.
Mix sugar and flour, add egg yolk and 1 tablespoon milk to make a smooth paste. Bring the milk and juice to the boil and pour over the blended mixture, whisking well. Return to the saucepan and cook gently until thick, stirring all the time. Cool.
Divide the filling equally between the pastry cases. Place drained apricot halves on top and bake in a fairly hot oven, 375°F or Gas Mark 5, for about 15 minutes on the second top shelf. For the glaze, bring jam and water to the boil for a few minutes, stirring all the time. Sieve and brush over the hot tarts.

Domino Sponges

6 ounces margarine
6 ounces caster sugar
3 eggs
6 ounces self-raising flour

ICING:
8 ounces icing sugar
warm water
2 ounces plain chocolate

Cream fat and sugar until light and fluffy. Add eggs one at a time and beat well. Add 1 teaspoon flour with the third egg. Sieve the flour into the mixture and pour into a greased swiss roll tin. Cook for 20 minutes in hot oven, 400°F or Gas Mark 6, until golden brown. Turn out on to a wire tray and allow to cool.
Make up glacé icing and spread over the top. Allow to dry and cut into long strips with a dry, warm knife; then divide into pieces the size of a domino. Melt the chocolate in a double boiler and put into a greaseproof paper piping bag (see p. 73) and pipe domino dots on to the sponges. If you like, decorate one half of the sponges with chocolate icing and make dots with white icing.

Family Fruit Cake

8 ounces margarine
4 ounces soft brown sugar
4 level tablespoons golden syrup
grated rind of 2 lemons
4 eggs
2 ounces ground almonds
1 tablespoon sherry
8 ounces plain flour
pinch of salt
3 pounds mixed fruit
4 ounces mixed peel or cherries
2 teaspoons mixed spice
freshly grated nutmeg

Line and grease a 9-inch round or square tin. Cream margarine and sugar together until light and fluffy. Add lemon rinds. Sieve flour, salt and spice together. Beat in eggs one at a time, together with a little flour with the last two eggs. Add ground almonds and fold in fruit, flour and sherry. Spread into the tin and make a hollow in the centre. Tie a double piece of brown paper round the side and sit the cake on a sheet of double brown paper. Bake in the middle shelf of a cool oven, 300°F or Gas Mark 2, for 1 hour. Reduce the heat to 275°F or Gas Mark 1 and cook for a further 4 hours or until a skewer comes out clean. Allow to cool then turn out on to a tin or a wire tray. The cake will keep for weeks in an airtight tin.

Sunday Teas

CHEESE LOAF
CUCUMBER SANDWICHES
PINWHEEL SANDWICHES
SARDINE TOAST FINGERS
COFFEE WALNUT CAKE

Cheese Loaf

8 ounces self-raising flour
½ teaspoon salt
½ teaspoon mustard
pinch of cayenne pepper
2 ounces butter
3 ounces grated cheese
1 egg
2 tablespoons milk
2 tablespoons water

Sieve flour, salt, mustard and cayenne in a mixing bowl. Cut the butter into small pieces and rub in until getting a fine breadcrumb texture. Stir in cheese, egg, milk and water and mix into a soft dough. Place in a greased 1-pound tin. Bake in a moderate oven, 375°F or Gas Mark 5, for 45 minutes on the second shelf until golden brown. Allow to cool on a wire tray. Serve sliced with butter. It is also delicious toasted.

Cucumber Sandwiches

Thin slices of bread with crusts removed. Thinly sliced cucumber, seasoned.

Pinwheel Sandwiches

(as shown on p. 64)

FILLING:
2 ounces butter
8 ounces corn beef
a few drops of Worcester sauce
salt and pepper
5 olives for each slice

Cream butter with seasoning and mashed corn beef.

Ham and Asparagus Wheels

Mince or chop ham and cream with the butter. Spread on the bread and round a piece of asparagus.

Sardine Fingers

1 ounce butter
½ teaspoon curry powder
1 can sardines
slices of toast

Spread the toast with creamed butter and curry powder. Cut into fingers. Place one sardine on each finger. Heat for a few minutes and serve.

Coffee Walnut Cake

Victoria sandwich recipe as for Domino Sponges on p. 61, *plus:*

2 tablespoons instant coffee
3 tablespoons warm water

Add coffee, made up in water, after the fat and sugar have been creamed. Proceed as for Domino Sponges.
Divide mixture into two 7-inch sandwich tins and cook in the centre of a moderate oven, 350°F or Gas Mark 4, for 20-25 minutes. Allow to cool for a few minutes and then place on a wire tray to cool.

Coffee Cream

2 ounces butter
4 ounces icing sugar
1 tablespoon instant coffee,
 mixed with
1 tablespoon warm water
8 walnuts, finely chopped

Cream the icing sugar, coffee and butter together. Stir in walnuts. Use mixture to sandwich the two cakes together.

Coffee Frosting

1 pound granulated sugar
12 tablespoons water
1 teaspoon instant coffee, made up in
2 teaspoons water
2 egg whites

Put the sugar and water in a thick saucepan and allow to dissolve over a low heat. Brush down any crystals which appear above the level of

the liquid. *Do not stir*. When the sugar has dissolved, add the coffee liquid and allow to boil fast, again without stirring. Boil to 240°F if you have a sugar thermometer or until the sugar just begins to spin a 6-inch thread. Whisk the egg white until stiff and peaky. Pour on the hot syrup in a thin stream, holding the pan at a good height and whisking briskly all the time. When the icing begins to look like slightly shiny cotton wool, spread quickly on the cake with sweeping strokes. Decorate the sides of the cake with halved walnuts.

Here you see the final stage in the preparation of the frosting. The egg white is whisked with the syrup. Remember to work quickly once the frosting is made.

Fill the inside of the cake first before beginning the frosting then put a thin coat over the sides to make sure there are no stray crumbs. Lastly decorate the top.

Party Sandwiches

Here you see the long slices of bread rolled out and spread with filling. The olives are placed in position and the pinwheels are ready to be rolled.

Roll the bread tightly, wrap in tinfoil or greaseproof and only slice into rings when you want to use them.

Remove the crusts from a brown and white loaf. Cut slices lengthwise.

Ribbon Sandwiches: Alternate 2 long slices whole-wheat and 2 white to make a Ribbon Loaf. Slice crosswise for "ribbons".

Checkerboards: Make Ribbon loaves. Cut in 6 *lengthwise* slices; put 4 slices together alternating colours. Chill; slice crosswise.

For the Open Sandwiches above

For the boatshapes:
Take square pieces of brown bread and remove the crusts. Spread with butter and slices of meat. Join two corners of the bread together with a cocktail stick with an olive. Smoked salmon is an excellent filling, sprinkle with lemon juice and paprika.

To fill the open squares:
Cut the square of bread into quarters, spread with a cream cheese or mayonnaise and egg filling, decorate with squares of green pepper.

For the crescents:
You can cut your sandwiches into any shape by cutting the bread with shaped biscuit cutters. This is especially good for small children if they won't eat bread they may eat a buttered rabbit or duck shape.

For the coronets:
Wrap buttered bread into a coronet shape, fill with a creamy savoury filling, e.g. tuna fish and mayonnaise, secure with a cocktail stick.

c

CHAPTER 6

Teenage Parties

When your children outgrow animal biscuits and gingerbread men, they will hanker for more savoury and sophisticated food for their entertaining.

Colourful presentation means a lot to teenagers as they are at an impressionable age.

For the younger teenagers, you need look no further than coke for the accompanying drink.

For the eighteen-year-old, the question of alcoholic refreshment need not be a problem if handled sensibly. Attractive wine and cider cups provide all the elements of excitement with a relatively low alcoholic content.

For the more sophisticated and older teenagers, try a Cheese Fondue Party.

Cheese Fondue

1½ pounds Gruyère cheese
8 ounces Emmenthal cheese
1 clove garlic
⅓ bottle Spanish chablis
¼ teaspoon grated nutmeg
freshly ground black pepper
1½ tablespoons Kirsch
cornflour
French bread

Snacks by the yard.
Use your own favourite combinations.

Crush clove of garlic, add to wine, bring to the boil and reduce slightly. Stir in the grated cheese, nutmeg and pepper over a low heat. Keep stirring until cheese is melted. Thicken with cornflour until mixture will easily coat bread. Transfer to fondue dish. Add Kirsch and have everyone standing at the ready with pieces of bread. To follow the fondue, serve fresh fruit or fruit salad (see p. 88).

On a less exotic note, the following variations on old established favourites, will satisfy young and hearty appetites.

Snacks by the Yard

Cut a long French loaf in two, after warming it in the oven. Spread with butter.

This is a bake bean base.
Use mustard sauce from page 15.

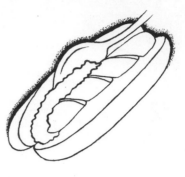

HOT DOGS

Preheat electric frying pan to 250°F (or use ordinary pan on medium heat). Cook onion in hot fat until tender, but not brown.

Stir in ketchup, water, vinegar, sugar, relish and seasoning. For fancy sausages, cut very lightly round the sausage. Add to sauce in pan; lower temperature to 220°F.

Cover and simmer for about 15 minutes until heated through. Slice and toast rolls; butter. Spoon sausages and sauce into rolls. Makes 8-10 servings.

TOPPINGS:

1) Hamburger mixture (see below) cooked and spread on the bread. Garnish with cheese slices cut into triangles, and slices of tomato.

2) Baked beans as a bed covered with gherkins and frankfurters or pork sausages. Split the sausages and squeeze mustard through the middle.

3) Chive Scrambled Eggs and Bacon Rolls. Cook 3 eggs, $\frac{1}{4}$ pint milk, seasoning, $\frac{1}{2}$ teaspoon chives and 1 ounce butter in a double boiler until thick, stirring occasionally. Make a bacon roll for each person and cook in the oven. Alternate with wedges of tomato.

Chilli Hamburger

8 round rolls or buns
1$\frac{1}{2}$ ounces cooking fat
8 ounces minced beef
2 ounces fresh white breadcrumbs
1 small onion, finely chopped
1 teaspoon tomato purée
$\frac{1}{2}$ teaspoon chilli powder
1 teaspoon Worcester sauce
salt and pepper

Mix the meat mixture and separate into eight portions. Leave in the refrigerator to firm. Fry until golden brown and cooked through. Heat the rolls in a hot oven for a few minutes, split and fill with the hamburgers.

Burgundy Beefburgers

1$\frac{1}{2}$ pounds minced beef
4 ounces soft breadcrumbs
1 egg
2 tablespoons red wine
salt and pepper
2 tablespoons spring onions, sliced
2 ounces butter
4 tablespoons red wine
6 thick slices French bread
   (cut diagonally)

Mix the beef, breadcrumbs, egg, red wine and seasoning in a bowl. Cook the green onions in butter until tender, then add 4 tablespoons wine. Grill the meat mixture until done, brushing over with sauce frequently. Place on buttered slices of French bread. Serve remaining sauce with the burgers.

Burger Mountains

Serve two burgers, the bottom one half-an-inch larger than the top to make a mountain. Use cucumber and tomato slices to separate burgers. Spear with a cocktail stick, skewered with olive and onion.

Square Burgers

Make squares of meat from the recipe in previous column. Serve on squares of toasted bread with deep fried onion rings.

Gnocchi Romana

5 ounces(tablespoons)semolina
1 pint milk
1 onion
2-3 cloves
6 peppercorns
1 bay leaf
½ ounce butter
salt and pepper
1 teaspoon prepared mustard
3 ounces cheese
1 ounce cheese

Pour milk into a saucepan. Add the onion stuck with cloves, bay leaf and peppercorns. Cover and heat gently for at least 10 minutes. Strain milk into a clean saucepan, bring just to boiling point then whisk in the semolina and stir frequently for a few minutes over a low heat. Add seasoning, cheese and butter and continue stirring until the cheese is melted. Do not allow to boil. Turn on to wet baking sheet or flat dish spread ¾-inch thick. Leave to cool. Cut into squares, dipping the knife into cold water to prevent sticking. Arrange on a buttered dish and sprinkle with cheese and dot with butter. Reheat in the oven and finish under the grill.

Fried Gnocchi

Make the Gnocchi as in the previous recipe but spread at least 1-inch thick to cool. Cut into small squares or fingers, lightly flour and then egg-and-crumb before frying in deep or shallow fat.

Rum Sweets

4 ounces biscuit crumbs
3 ounces seedless raisins
1 ounce icing sugar
½ tablespoon cocoa
2 tablespoons rum
2 ounces walnuts
2 ounces syrup
2 ounces butter, melted

Crush biscuits in a greaseproof bag with a rolling pin. Chop raisins and nuts finely. Mix ingredients together and roll into balls with the hands. Roll in icing sugar. Place in small sweet papers.

Cherry Bon Bons

24 maraschino cherries
6 tablespoons brandy
3 ounces dipping chocolate

Allow cherries to stand in brandy for a few hours. Drain and allow to dry. Melt chocolate in a bowl over hot water. Dip cherries in and remove on to a tray lined with foil.

Almond Chocolates

2 ounces almonds, finely chopped
2 ounces caster sugar
1 egg yolk
4 ounces milk chocolate
1 tablespoon water

Grate the chocolate, add half to the almonds together with the yolks, water and sugar. Blend into a firm, workable paste. Shape into balls the size of cherries and roll in the grated chocolate.

Drinks

A hot mulled wine (see p. 20) is an excellent drink to serve with the fondue. You might also try the following Cider Cup or Hot Punch.

Cider Cup

3 pints cider
2 pints lemonade
1 pint undiluted lemon squash

Mix cider, lemonade and squash. Pour over chopped apple, sliced oranges and mint leaves. Chill before serving.

Hot Punch

4 pints dry cider
3 tablespoons granulated sugar
3 tablespoons brown sugar
1 tablespoon grated lemon rind
1 teaspoon allspice
1 small stick cinnamon
½ teaspoon cloves

Burgundy Beefburger
Burger Mountain
Square Burger

Put all the ingredients in a pan, mix well, bring to the boil and allow to simmer for about 20 minutes. Strain into a bowl and serve hot.

Devonshire Punch

3 pints apple juice
juice of 6 oranges
12 cloves
(¼ pint brandy can be added if an
    alcoholic beverage is required)

Mix all the ingredients together and serve very cold with ice.

Banana Splits

1 banana per person
1 scoop vanilla ice cream
4 ounces melted chocolate
1 jelly, made up and set
chopped nuts
whipped cream

Divide banana lengthwise, put ice cream between with chopped jelly at each side, pour over a little chocolate. Sprinkle with chopped nuts and add whipped cream.

Chocolate Cherry Cake

4 large eggs
8 ounces caster sugar
8 ounces unsalted butter
8 ounces plain chocolate
8 ounces plain sieved flour

Left: Devonshire Punch

Right: Chocolate Cherry Cake

Beat eggs and sugar until light and fluffy, and until the volume has trebled. Soften butter and chocolate in a double boiler and add the egg mixture. Sieve flour and fold in well. Cook in two greased 7-inch cake tins in a moderate oven, 350°F or Gas Mark 4, for about 25 minutes. Allow to cool in the tin for a few minutes and turn out on to a wire tray.

FILLING:
1 can Cherry Pie Filling

Icing

6 ounces icing sugar
2 ounces butter
1 tablespoon cocoa
2 tablespoons warm water

Cream fat until soft. Add 1 tablespoon icing sugar, blend in cocoa with water and gradually add the rest of the icing sugar, beating until you have a fluffy icing. Fill chocolate cakes with cherry filling, sandwich together, cover the sides with butter icing, roll in chopped chocolate or milk flake.

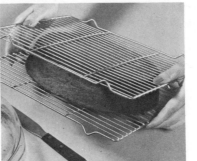

Put your tins into the middle shelf of the oven.

Tip cake out on to a wire rack. Turn onto another rack so that top surface does not mark.

Battenberg Cake

1 Domino sponge mixture (see p. 61)
Apricot Jam

Almond Paste
4 ounces ground almonds
2 ounces caster sugar
½ egg
1 teaspoon lemon juice
2 ounces icing sugar

Mix the caster and icing sugar with the ground almonds. Add the half egg lightly beaten. Work to a smooth paste.
The above quantities make enough paste for the Battenberg cake.

To make up Battenberg Cake

Line a greased swiss roll tin. Take a 2-inch band of greaseproof paper or aluminium foil to fit down the centre. Make the Victoria Sandwich mixture. Put half the mixture down one side of the tin. Place the band of paper down the centre. Colour the second half of the mixture pink, green, or chocolate, and put it into the other half of the tin. Bake for about 12 minutes at 400°F or Gas Mark 6. Turn the cake on to a wire tray. Remove the paper when cool. There are now two long strips of cake, one plain and one coloured. Halve each piece. Put a plain square alongside a coloured oblong and stick them together with jam. Spread the top surfaces with jam and place the two remaining squares of cake on top, putting the coloured squares on to the plain one and the plain one on to the coloured one. Spread the top and sides of the cake with sieved jam, and then cover with thinly rolled almond paste. Finish by pinching the edges with finger and thumb and scoring the top of the cake.

Boston Coffee Creams

These delicious biscuits are made from a rich mixture. The following ingredients make 2-3 dozen biscuits.

5 ounces plain flour
4 ounces margarine or butter
1 ounce icing sugar
¼ teaspoon vanilla essence
½ egg

Cream the fat and sugar together. Beat the egg, add half of it with the vanilla essence. Mix in the sieved flour. Put the mixture into a forcing bag with a large rosette pipe. Pipe on to a greased baking tray. Bake for 15 minutes in a moderate oven, 350°F, or Gas Mark 4. Cool and sandwich together with coffee butter icing.

Chocolate Cookies

5 ounces plain flour
4 ounces margarine
2 ounces caster sugar
½ teaspoon vanilla essence
½ level teaspoon salt
6 ounces either milk or plain chocolate
2 ounces sweet almonds
1 egg
1 ounce flour for rolling

Blanch and skin the almonds. Rinse, then dry them in a cloth. Chop fairly coarsely. Roughly chop the chocolate. Sieve flour, rub in margarine until mixture resembles fine breadcrumbs. Add vanilla, salt, chopped nuts and chocolate for the top of the cookies. Mix in the beaten egg. Form into small balls and place on a greased baking sheet. Place a piece of chocolate and nut on top of each ball. Bake in a preheated oven, 350°F, or Gas Mark 4, for 10-15 minutes. Cool on wire tray. Store in an airtight tin.

CHAPTER 7

Toddlers Parties

Name Biscuits

8 ounces plain flour
4 ounces fine semolina
pinch of salt
8 ounces butter or margarine
4 ounces caster sugar

Sieve flour, semolina and salt. Cream fat and sugar until soft and fluffy. Add dry ingredients. Roll out half the mixture to $\frac{1}{4}$-inch thick and cut into rounds with a biscuit cutter. Prick and bake in a moderate oven, 350°F or Gas Mark 4, for 20 minutes until golden brown. Cut the remaining mixture into animal shapes and cook in the same way.

Pink Icing

4 ounces icing sugar
1 ounce margarine

Decorating tube (a cone of greaseproof paper will do) and icing make names on top of the biscuits.

1 tablespoon milk
pink colouring

Flowerpot Cookie Cups made from puffed rice cereal, fill with favourite flavours of ice cream to make a special treat for a toddler's party. Lollipops are good, also. Serve with mugs of hot chocolate or milk.

This jumbo cake has a parade of animal biscuits marching round the edge. Insert tiny candles in snipped marshmallows and light just before serving. Arrange animals on a large biscuit on round piece of sponge using the icing given above.

Cream fat, add icing sugar gradually until you have a soft cream icing. Pipe names on to the biscuits.
Fill cone with icing and pipe names on the biscuits.

Make a paper cone by cutting a 12-inch square of greaseproof paper.

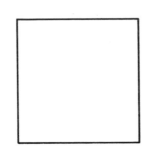

Fold Paper into a Triangle

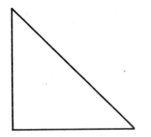

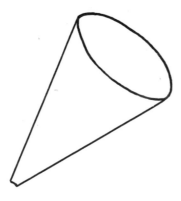

Fold into a Coronet. Cut off a small tip

Flowerpot Cookie Cups

**Rice crispies
8 ounces large marshmallows
2 ounces butter
Chocolate Ice Cream (see p. 15)
Lollipops
Ice Cream Cones**

Place rice crispies in shallow pan in moderate oven, 350°F or Gas Mark 4, for 10 minutes. Turn into a large, greased bowl. Melt marshmallows and butter over a very low heat, stirring till smooth.
Pour marshmallow mixture over cereal, mixing until all the cereal is coated. Press into bottom and sides of ten greased dariole moulds or patty tins. If mixture cools too fast, return to oven and heat slightly. Cool; remove from cups; fill with chocolate ice cream (or a combination of favourite flavours). Use ice cream cones as clown hats stuck on top of ice cream *or* lollipops.

Crispy Chocolate Cakes

**8 ounces chocolate
1 ounce raisins
corn flakes
paper cases**

Melt the chocolate in a large bowl over hot water, add the raisins, then sprinkle in enough corn flakes to be thoroughly coated with the chocolate. Spoon into paper cases and allow to set.

Toddlers Sandwiches

**Thinly sliced brown and white bread
Butter
Jam, honey or other favourite fillings**

Cut the bread in animal shapes; e.g. using two ducks, one brown one white, for each sandwich. Even the older children enjoy these shaped sandwiches.

CHAPTER 8

Childrens Parties

Ranch Birthday Cake

Make 2 mixtures of:
   6 ounces butter or margarine
   6 ounces caster sugar
   3 eggs
   6 ounces self-raising flour
Chocolate filling:
   8 ounces chocolate
   2 egg yolks
   2 ounces butter

Cream butter and sugar until light, creamy and fluffy. Cream in 1 heaped teaspoon cocoa mixed with 2 tablespoons warm water with the second cake mixture. Add eggs, one at a time with a little flour and beat thoroughly. Sieve flour into the mixture and fold in with a spoon. Cook in a moderate oven, 375°F or Gas Mark 5, for 20 minutes in a greased swiss roll tin. You now have one chocolate and one white oblong sponge. Allow to cool and then halve the cakes so that you have four layers. Sandwich alternate brown and white layers with the chocolate filling. Decorate the cake with butter icing (see p. 71) coloured to your preference, and using 8-10 ounces icing sugar. Liquorice can be used to make the brand marks or they can be piped.

Happy Birthday Cake

Make one mixture as used in Ranch House Birthday Cake (see above). Allow to cool. Cut into strips and then into small cakes of an even rectangular shape.
Place on a wire tray.
Make up glacé icing with warm water and spoon over. Have at least three different colours of iced cakes.
e.g. to have HAPPY BIRTHDAY MARY you will need 17 small cakes. Pipe round the edge of the little cakes with butter icing or royal icing. Then write one letter on each cake. Arrange on a tray. Decorate the corners with flowers and put the candles on some of the name cakes.

Birthday Cake

(Traditional Fruit Cake Recipe)

6 ounces butter
6 ounces caster sugar
4 eggs
6 ounces currants
4 ounces sultanas
3 ounces raisins
2 ounces chopped peel
1 ounce cherries
rind of 1 lemon
4 ounces self-raising flour
4 ounces plain flour
pinch of salt
$\frac{1}{2}$ teaspoon nutmeg
$\frac{1}{2}$ teaspoon cinnamon

Cream fat and sugar together until light and fluffy. Beat eggs into the mixture one by one (add a little flour with the last two, if necessary). Sieve in the flour and fold in with a metal spoon. Fold in the fruit and turn into a lined 8-inch cake tin. Tie a band of brown paper outside the cake and stand the cake tin on a piece of brown paper in the oven. Bake for about 3—4 hours at 300°F or Gas Mark 2.
Decorate with Almond Paste (see p. 56) and Royal Icing (see below) or Frosting (see p. 78).

Royal Icing

1$\frac{1}{2}$ pounds icing sugar
3 egg whites
1 teaspoon lemon juice
1 teaspoon glycerine

Do not use eggs straight from the refrigerator; allow them to return to room temperature before using. Sieve the icing sugar into a bowl. Put the separated egg whites into a basin and beat until just frothy. Gradually beat in half the icing sugar to the egg whites with a wooden spoon. Keep on beating until the icing is fluffy; this may take 5 minutes or more. Add the lemon juice and glycerine then mix in remaining icing a little at a time. When the icing peaks, enough icing sugar has been added. It is best to leave the icing covered over with a damp cloth for at least half-an-hour before using. Cover over any remaining icing after decorating.

Boys have an unfortunate habit of requesting odd cakes and I had to cope recently with a request for a football cake from my son. Here it is.

Football Cake

1 cake mixture (see Birthday Cake), cooked in 2 greased pudding tins (mixture will take about 2$\frac{1}{2}$ hours to cook)
1 cake board covered with butter icing (see p. 71) coloured for the appropriate team
12 ounces almond paste (1$\frac{1}{2}$ times the recipe for Simnel Cake recipe p. 56), with 2 tablespoons cocoa added to the icing sugar before you make the paste
apricot jam, warmed and sieved
Royal Icing (see above made up with 1 egg white instead of 3)

Cut a piece from one side of each cake so that the football will stand up. Sandwich cakes together by brushing the tops with apricot jam and then using a thin piece of almond paste the same size as the surface. Leave to firm for a while. Roll out the almond paste and brush the cake all over with apricot jam. Cover the cake, smoothing with your hands. Put on the covered board and mark the seams of the ball with a pastry wheel. Pipe the boy's name and age on the side. Pipe an outline of the lacing at the top of the ball. Pipe round the bottom of the cake to cover the join between the cake and the board. Put candles at each end like goal posts.

These recipes are a firm favourite with growing boys and girls and are ideal as an alternative to the less satisfying sandwich.

Meat & Bean Pie

8 ounces flaky pastry (see p. 49)
1 pound minced beef
$\frac{1}{2}$ ounce butter
1 onion, finely chopped
salt and pepper
1 teaspoon Worcester sauce
$\frac{1}{4}$ pint stock or water
1 large can baked beans

Sauté the onion in butter, brown minced beef,

Childrens Parties

Making animal biscuits can be
fun for everyone.

Meat Pie

**8 ounces short crust pastry (see p. 43,
  cheese can be omitted)**
1 pound minced beef
1 ounce fat
$\frac{1}{4}$ onion, finely chopped
$\frac{1}{4}$ pint stock or water
salt and pepper
**1 dessertspoon tomato ketchup or
  purée**

Cook the minced beef and onion in the fat
until meat is brown. Add tomato purée,
seasoning and stock. Simmer gently for 10-15
minutes and allow to cool. Line a flan ring or
sandwich cake tin with two-thirds of the
pastry; fill with meat mixture. Roll out remaining
one-third of pastry to cover the top. Seal the
edges, cut slits on the top to allow the steam
to escape. Cook in hot oven, 400°F or Gas
Mark 6, for 20-25 minutes.

If you don't want to serve a cooked tea I am
told no party is complete without small
sausages on sticks. If you can't buy them, try
ordinary sized chipolatas, twist them in the
middle and—hey presto—a small cocktail
sausage!

Chocolate Animal Biscuits

8 ounces plain flour
pinch of salt
1 tablespoon cocoa
4 ounces butter or caster sugar
1 beaten egg to mix

Sieve flour, salt and cocoa into a bowl. Rub
fat in until mixture resembles fine breadcrumbs.
Add the sugar and the egg to mix. Roll out and
cut with animal shapes. Bake in a moderate
oven 350°F or Gas Mark 4, for 10 minutes or
until cooked through.

add seasoning and water. Simmer for 10
minutes. Pour the beans into the bottom of a
pie-dish or oblong ovenproof dish and spoon
the onion/meat mixture over the beans. Roll
out pastry thinly and cover the pie. Brush with
beaten egg, mark out the portions without
cutting through the pastry and cook in a very
hot oven, 450°F or Gas Mark 8, until pastry has
turned pale golden brown and has risen.

Orange Parasol Cake

6 ounces margarine
6 ounces caster sugar
3 eggs
2 tablespoons orange juice
rind of 1 orange
6 ounces self-raising flour

Cream fat and sugar until a light fluffy texture. Add orange rind and gradually add eggs one by one with a little flour. Sieve in the flour and fold into the mixture. Add 2 tablespoons juice at the end. Turn into 2 7-inch sandwich tins and bake in the middle of the shelf in a moderate oven, 350°F or Gas Mark 4, for 25 minutes.

Fluffy White Frosting

8 ounces granulated sugar
3 tablespoons water
$\frac{1}{4}$ teaspoon cream of tartar
pinch of salt
2 unbeaten egg whites
a few drops of orange juice

Combine sugar, water, cream of tartar and salt in a saucepan. Dissolve sugar slowly then bring to the boil. Slowly add the mixture to the unbeaten egg whites and beat with a whisk or electric mixer until peaks form.

The parasols can be bought in the larger stationery shops.

Parasol Cake is popular
with little girls.

Gingerbread Men cause great
hilarity at childrens' parties.

Gingerbread Men

8 ounces plain flour
3 teaspoons ground ginger
1 teaspoon mixed spice
2½ ounces margarine
2 tablespoons golden syrup
2 ounces granulated sugar
1 teaspoon bicarbonate soda
1 dessertspoon water

Sieve flour (keeping a little aside for the rolling out of the mixture), ginger and mixed spice into a bowl. Melt margarine, golden syrup and sugar in a saucepan without boiling. Allow to cool slightly before using. Then pour into the flour. Dissolve bicarbonate of soda in the water and stir into the other ingredients. Flour a rolling pin and board. Knead mixture, and roll out thinly. Cut out with the cardboard shaped man or gingerbread man cutter. Currants can be used for eyes and mouth or these can be piped on after baking with chocolate or icing. Cook for 10-12 minutes in a moderate oven, 350°F or Gas Mark 4.

This sweet made with jelly and
ice cream is a winner with children.

Nutty Toffee Apples

1 pound sugar
6 tablespoons water
2 teaspoons vinegar
chopped nuts optional

Dissolve sugar slowly in the liquid then boil until the toffee begins to thicken and brown. A spot of red colouring may be added before dipping the apples. After dipping in toffee, dip the bottom in chopped nuts.

Nutty Toffee apples

CHAPTER 9

Special Occasion

Anniversary Dinner

For 8 servings

FLORIDA COCKTAIL
SOLE SURPRISE
CHICKEN IN WINE VINEGAR
or **CHICKEN FINANZIERA**
   POTATO SOUFFLÉ
   BROCCOLI
CHOCOLATE MOUSSE

Florida Cocktail

   4 grapefruits
   4 oranges
   1 pint water
   6 ounces sugar
   juice of 1 lemon

Dip the grapefruit and oranges in boiling water for a few minutes, then peel removing all the white pith. Use a sharp knife to cut into sections so that the skin inside the fruit is left behind. Boil sugar, lemon juice and water together until it is reduced by half. Allow to cool. Pour over fruit. Arrange in dishes. Decorate with maraschino cherry and chill before serving.

Sole Surprise

   32 grapes: 24 peeled and seeded
   8 fillets of sole (keep trimmings)
   $\frac{1}{4}$ pint white wine
   $\frac{1}{4}$ pint water
   1 onion stuck with 2 cloves
   6 peppercorns
   $\frac{1}{4}$ pint thin cream

Season the fillets and roll three grapes in each fillet. Place the rolled fish in a buttered dish with the fish trimmings, wine, water, onion and peppercorns. Cover the dish and place in a fairly hot oven, 375°F or Gas Mark 5, for 20 minutes. Remove fish and arrange each fillet on a buttered scallop shell. Continue to simmer stock for another $\frac{1}{2}$ hour. Melt 1 ounce butter and add 1 ounce flour, make a *roux* and add the strained fish stock. Season, allow to cool slightly and add the cream. Pour over the fish and garnish with halved grapes, peeled and seeded.

Chicken in Wine Vinegar

   2 (3-pound) chicken
   3 ounces butter
   2 cloves garlic
   3 teaspoons French mustard
   1 tablespoon tomato purée
   $1\frac{1}{2}$ tablespoons white wine
   4 tablespoons wine vinegar
   1 tablespoon thick cream
   1 teaspoon Worcester sauce
   salt and pepper

Cut the chicken into 8 pieces and cook in a heavy covered pan with butter, unpeeled garlic and seasoning for about 25 minutes until chicken is cooked. Mix the mustard, tomato purée and white wine. When the chicken is cooked, add the vinegar and cook the chicken until almost dry. Take out the chicken and keep warm on a serving dish. Pour mustard/tomato mixture into the pan and reduce a little without the cover. Stir in the cream and Worcester sauce. Pour over the chicken.

Potato Soufflé

   8 medium-sized potatoes
   3 ounces butter
   generous $\frac{1}{4}$ pint scalded milk
   3 egg yolks
   3 egg whites, stiffly beaten
   salt and pepper

Cover the washed potatoes with cold salted water. Bring to a boil, cook and drain, peel the potatoes, and mash thoroughly. Beat in the

Chocolate Mousse
attractively
served in
individual pots.

butter and milk, using a wire whisk. Season and still whisking, add the egg yolks, one by one, beating hard after each. Fold in the egg whites. Butter a soufflé or other straight-sided baking dish. Put the potato mixture and bake in a 425°F or Gas Mark 7 oven, for 20 to 25 minutes or until golden brown.

Broccoli

There are several varieties of this vegetables, the chief one being: White broccoli, with a fairly large flower head, which is cooked and served in the same way as cauliflower. Buy by the head and cook like a cauliflower, but takes only 15-20 minutes. Serve plain, buttered or with Hollandaise sauce.

If you would like an alternative chicken dish, try this delicious Italian recipe.

Chicken Finanziera

1 (4-pound) chicken, cut into portions
2 chicken livers
6 tablespoons olive oil
3 tablespoons celery, chopped
2 tablespoons parsley, finely chopped
pinch of basil

1 small onion, thinly sliced
1 carrot, diced
1 tablespoon flour
4 tablespoons chicken stock
8 tablespoons red wine
4 ounces mushrooms, sliced
8 tablespoons dry Marsala
salt and pepper

Cook the vegetables and basil in the oil, using a casserole, under a gentle heat until the onions begin to glaze. Add the chicken and cook for 15 minutes. Then remove and sieve the sauce. Put the sieved sauce back in the casserole, add flour and stir well. Gradually add the stock and wine, stirring gently all the time, and bring to the boil. Return the chicken, season and cook gently fpr another 20 minutes. Remove chicken and keep warm. Add mushrooms, livers and Marsala. Simmer for a little over 5 minutes and pour over the chicken.

Chocolate Mousse

8 ounces bitter chocolate
8 eggs
4 ounces sugar
2 tablespoons Grande Marnier

Melt chocolate over hot water. Mix the liqueur with the egg yolks and add gradually to the chocolate. Allow to cool. Beat up egg whites until stiff and add gently. Chill in individual dishes.

Birthday Dinner Party

TARAMASALATA   *For 8-10 servings*
  TOAST FINGERS
ITALIAN ROAST BEEF
  JACKET POTATOES (see p. 31)
  ZUCCHINI
PINEAPPLE MERINGUE BASKETS

Taramasalata

8 ounces smoked cod's roe
1 large potato, boiled and sieved
2 tablespoons water
juice of 1 lemon
freshly ground pepper
4 tablespoons oil
parsley

Mix the mashed potato with the roe until well blended. Add lemon juice and water, alternately with the oil, beating all the time until mixture becomes thick and creamy. Put into a dish, garnish with parsley and chill before serving.

Suggested Wines

Côtes de nuits or Beaujolais with the main course.

Italian Roast Beef

5 pounds rolled topside
1 large clove garlic
6 tablespoons oil
4 tablespoons cognac
salt and pepper

MARINADE:
$\frac{1}{4}$ pint red wine
sprig of rosemary (or $\frac{1}{2}$ teaspoon dried)
sprig of thyme (or $\frac{1}{2}$ teaspoon dried)
parsley
4 tablespoons oil

Pour marinade over the meat in a polythene bag, seal and leave for several hours. Remove from the marinade, reserve liquid and rub beef with crushed garlic, salt and pepper. Place in a roasting tin, paint with oil and then pour over warmed brandy. Flame and season again. Roast in a moderate oven, 350°F or Gas Mark 4, for 1 hour 20 minutes, underdone; 1 hour 45 minutes, medium. Baste the meat from time to time.
For the gravy:
Pour off the fat, stir in 1 dessertspoon cornflour, salt and pepper, and a little of the strained marinade with $\frac{1}{4}$ pint stock.

Zucchini (baby marrows)

2 pounds baby marrows
2 ounces butter
2 tablespoons olive oil
1 ounce white breadcrumbs
1 dessertspoon Parmesan cheese
salt and freshly ground black pepper
juice of 1 lemon

Wash the baby marrows and slice. Leave in a covered collander, sprinkled with salt and lemon juice for $\frac{1}{2}$ hour. Heat the butter and oil and sauté the baby marrows until golden brown. Arrange in a dish, sprinkle with crumbs and cheese mixed together and dot with butter. Finish in the oven or under the grill until the topping is golden brown.

Pineapple Meringue Baskets

For two baskets:
6 eggs
12 ounces caster sugar
pinch of salt
1 large can pineapple pieces
12 maraschino cherries
$\frac{1}{2}$ pint thick cream

Whisk egg whites until light and fluffy. Gradually whisk in two-thirds of the caster sugar until meringue is smooth, glossy and stands in peaks. Fold in remaining caster sugar and pipe on to a greased piece of tin foil or lined baking sheet. Start in the centre of a circle and pipe round and round until you arrive at the correct size. Pipe a double wall on the edge. Put in a very cool oven, 200°F or Gas Mark $\frac{1}{4}$, for several hours until dry and firm. Fill with whipped cream, pineapple (fresh if possible) and decorate with the cherries.

Use fresh herbs for your marinade if you have them. A polythene bag is ideal to marinade a large piece of meat as it allows the marinade to cover more of the meat.

Engagement Party

If you have more than 20 guests, I suggest you use one of the buffet menus given at the beginning of the book.

If it is a family affair, you could use the Anniversary Dinner or one of the Family Dinners.

However, if you have enough room to entertain 20 people, try the following menu. It may be possible to hire or borrow square folding tables to seat the multitude.

This is much more intimate and far less expensive than a party in a hotel—even if you hire a waitress.

All the dishes can be prepared well in advance and can be served from the cooker to the table.

For 20 servings

CREAM OF ASPARAGUS SOUP
SCALLOP PROVENÇAL (in tomato)
FILET DE BOEUF WELLINGTON
   (beef in pastry)
   POTATOES WITH CHEESE & CREAM
   MADEIRA SAUCE
   MIXED GREEN SALAD (see page 8)
KIRSCH TORTE
FRESH FRUIT
A SELECTION OF CHEESES

Asparagus Soup

   2 pounds fresh asparagus
   1 onion, finely chopped
   4 ounces butter
   2 bay leaves
   1 large sprig parsley
   small sprig basil
   4 pints chicken stock
   $\frac{1}{2}$ pint milk
   $2\frac{1}{2}$ ounces flour
   salt and pepper
   $\frac{1}{2}$ pint thick cream

Sweat onion in 2 ounces butter. Wash and trim asparagus, reserving the tips for a garnish. Add chopped stalks and sauté for a few minutes. Pour in stock and herbs. Bring to the boil and simmer for 1 hour. Sieve or liquidise the soup. Melt remaining butter in the rinsed soup pan, add flour and make a *roux*. Add soup and milk. Adjust the seasoning. Add cream and asparagus tips before serving.

Scallops Provençal

   20 scallops
   $\frac{1}{2}$ bottle dry white wine
   2 tablespoons oil
   1 large onion, finely chopped
   4 cloves garlic
   2 large cans tomatoes, peeled Italian
   salt or freshly ground black pepper
   chopped parsley

Take the scallops from their shells and remove yellowish beard (the fishmonger will do this for you if you ask nicely). Cook in a saucepan with the wine and seasoning for a few minutes. Remove scallops and reduce wine by half. Sweat onion and crushed garlic in oil for a few minutes. Drain tomatoes and chop. Then add to the onion and simmer mixture. Add wine liquor from the scallops. Check seasoning, add scallops and allow mixture to cool. Store in a cool place. Heat rapidly and simmer for a few minutes before serving in heated scallop shells. Sprinkle with chopped parsley.

Filet de Boeuf Wellington

   2 (4-5 pound) beef fillets
   8 ounces butter
   1 pound mushrooms
   $1\frac{1}{2}$ ounces butter
   2 onions, finely chopped
   1 tablespoon shallots, finely chopped
   6 ounces lean minced ham
   6 tablespoons tomato purée
   $\frac{3}{4}$ pint tomato juice
   5 pounds puff pastry (see p. 16)
   1 egg yolk

Prepare mushroom mixture by washing and chopping the mushrooms finely; squeezing in

kitchen paper to remove excess moisture; then cooking mushrooms in butter with onion and shallots until they begin to brown. Then add ham, tomato purée, salt and pepper.
Allow to simmer for a few minutes and set aside to cool.
Spread the two fillets with 4 ounces butter each. Season and brown in a very hot oven, 450°F or Gas Mark 8, for 25 minutes for under-done or 35 minutes for well done.
Allow to cool.
Roll the pastry into two oblongs about $\frac{1}{8}$-inch thick. Place the fillets in the centre and put half the mushroon mixture over each fillet. Fold up the pastry until the meat is completely covered. Seal the ends of the pastry by damping two edges and brush over with beaten egg. Cut strips of pastry with a pastry wheel and decorate the top. Place on baking sheets and prick the sides slightly to allow steam to escape. Store in the refrigerator.
When ready, cook in a hot oven, 425°F or Gas Mark 7, for about 20 minutes or until pastry is golden brown.
Carry into the dining room and serve by simply cutting the required number of slices. It looks good and tastes simply delicious. So easy to make, too.

Madeira Sauce

For 4 pints
    1 pint Madeira
    cooking juice from the steak
    3 pints beef stock
    2 tablespoons tomato purée
    salt and pepper
    4 ounces butter

Put the Madeira in a saucepan with the meat juice and reduce to half the volume. Add stock, tomato purée and boil for a few minutes. Remove from the heat, season and stir in butter. A few slices of mushroom can also be floated in the sauce.

Potatoes with Cheese and Cream

    5 pounds new potatoes
    2 pints milk
    salt and freshly ground black pepper
    butter
    1 pint cream
    12 tablespoons grated Gruyère cheese
    6 tablespoons freshly grated Parmesan

Peel and slice potatoes thinly; soak in cold water for a few minutes. Drain. Place the sliced potatoes in a heatproof buttered dish; add milk then season to taste with salt and pepper. Cook for 20 minutes or until half-done. Drain. Place drained potatoes in a clean buttered dish; add cream and sprinkle with the freshly grated cheeses. Dot with butter and cook in a moderate oven, 350°F or Gas Mark 4, for about 30 minutes . . . or until potatoes are cooked through. If top becomes brown, cover the dish with a foil. Serve very hot.

Suggested Wine

Pommerol or St. Emilion with the main course.

Kirsch Torte

For 3 cakes
    12 egg yolks
    1½ eggs
    8 ounces caster sugar
    4½ ounces sponge crumbs
    4½ ounces ground almonds
    2 ounces cocoa
    3 ounces flour
    8 egg whites
    1½ pounds Morella cherries, stoned
    2 teaspoons cornflour
    2 pints thick cream, whipped
    6 tablespoons Kirsch
    grated chocolate

Beat egg yolks and eggs with the sugar and 1 tablespoon warm water until thick. Add crumbs and ground almonds then the stiffly beaten egg whites, followed by sieved flour and cocoa. Pour mixture into three 7-inch greased and floured sandwich tins. Bake in a moderately hot oven, 375°F or Gas Mark 5. When baked and cooled, slice into three.
Bind two-thirds of the cherries with cornflour and cherry juice; chill. Put cherry mixture on the first layer, then sandwich remaining two layers with kirsch-flavoured whipped cream. Coat sides with cream and pipe cream on top. Decorate with remaining cherries and chocolate

With all this hard work behind you, all you have to do on the day is to serve the food, absolutely no cooking except what the oven does for you!

Wedding Buffet

Many people find the expense of outside wedding receptions too high and prefer to cater at home when it is a small reception for around 30 people. The wedding cake naturally takes pride of place so I deal with this first.

Wedding Cake

For a 12-inch square cake

$2\frac{1}{4}$ pounds butter
$1\frac{1}{2}$ pounds caster sugar
8 ounces soft brown sugar
2 tablespoons treacle
30 eggs
6 pounds currants
$1\frac{1}{2}$ pounds sultanas
$1\frac{1}{4}$ pounds cherries
$2\frac{3}{4}$ pounds raisins
12 ounces almonds
12 ounces chopped peel
rind of 6 lemons
3 pounds plain flour
$\frac{1}{2}$ teaspoon salt
3 teaspoons nutmeg
2 teaspoons mixed spice
1 teaspoon allspice
2 teaspoons cinnamon
$\frac{1}{4}$ pint brandy

If you do not want to make such a large quantity make the mixture in two halves. Use a large plastic basin for mixing the ingredients. Line a 12-inch cake tin with greaseproof paper and cut brown paper strips to go round the sides and a square piece for the cake to sit on when it is in the oven. For the Method, see Birthday Cake p. 76. When baking start at 300°F or Gas Mark 2 for 1 hour and then allow to cook for 7 hours at 275°F or Gas Mark 1. Store the cake wrapped in paper and a tea towel for some weeks to mature. Prick and drop in some brandy to the bottom before use.

Almond Paste

6 egg yolks
$1\frac{1}{2}$ pounds ground almonds
12 ounces caster sugar
12 ounces icing sugar
juice of 1 lemon

Chocolate Cream bun

See p. 56 for method.

Royal Icing

5 pounds icing sugar
12 egg whites
6 tablespoons lemon juice
6 teaspoons glycerine

See p. 76 for method.

If you are afraid of tackling the icing of the cake you can have it done by a professional for around £3.

LOBSTER COCKTAIL
PLATES OF:
   COLD ROAST BEEF
   COLD ROAST PORK
   TONGUE
     POTATO SALAD
     TOMATO VINAIGRETTE
     MIXED GREEN SALAD (see p. 8)
LARGE CHOCOLATE BUNS OR ÉCLAIRS
FRUIT SALAD

Lobster Cocktail

5 pounds lobster, cooked
2 large cans tomatoes
25 mushrooms
26 lettuce leaves
brandy
1½ pints mayonnaise, tomato flavoured

Drain the tomatoes and bind the tomato with the mayonnaise (see p. 18). Place the lettuce leaves in the bottom of the dishes (champagne glasses are ideal) and fill with the mixture. Garnish with sliced lobster and a mushroom. Sprinkle with a few drops of brandy.

Roast Beef (see p. 38)

Roast Pork

1 (5 pound) Leg of Pork, scored

Rub the outside fat with salt. Cook in a moderately hot oven, 375°F or Gas Mark 5, for 2½ hours.

Wedding Cake
cut ready
for serving
with champagne.

Ox Tongue

Soak the tongue in cold water for 24 hours. Change the water at least twice. Put the tongue in a saucepan of water which just covers it, together with 1 bay leaf, a sprig of parsley and 12 peppercorns. Bring to the boil and simmer for about three hours until the tip of the tongue seems tender. Allow to cool, skin and pack in a round dish. Reduce the cooking liquid by half and pour over. This will turn into jelly when the tongue is turned out of the dish. Put a heavy weight on top. Chill and turn out.

Suggested Wine

Blanc de blancs.

Potato Salad

10 pounds medium sized potatoes
1½ pints bouillon
1¼ pint vinaigrette sauce (see p. 8)
10 hard-boiled eggs
gherkin pickles
5 tablespoons chopped parsley
Mayonnaise (see p. 18)
salt and pepper

Cook the potatoes in their jackets in boiling salted water until just tender. Peel and slice thinly into a salad bowl. Season and pour boiling bouillon over them. Add the vinaigrette and mix. Top with sliced eggs, pickles and parsley. Serve mayonnaise separately.

Tomato Vinaigrette

25 tomatoes
3 onions
salt and pepper
vinaigrette sauce (see p. 8)
chives, tarragon and parsley

Dip the tomatoes into boiling water for a few seconds and then peel. Cut into slices. Arrange in a bowl with onion slices; season. Allow to stand for an hour, remove the onion and pour off the juice. Add the vinaigrette and chopped herbs.

Large Chocolate Buns

Make up 3 quantities of
Choux pastry:
½ pint water
pinch of salt
5 ounces butter
5 ounces plain flour
3 eggs

1½ pints thick cream, whipped

Chocolate Icing
3 rounded tablespoons cocoa
3 rounded tablespoons granulated sugar
3 tablespoons water
18 ounces icing sugar

Heat water and butter in a saucepan. When the water bubbles, add the sieved flour. Remove from the heat and beat immediately. Beat hard until mixture leaves the sides of the pan. Allow mixture to cool and beat in the eggs gradually. Pipe on to a greased sheet, either in 3-inch lengths for éclair shapes or in rounds. Bake in a hot oven, 400°F or Gas Mark 6, for about 30 minutes. Make a slit in each and return to the oven to dry for 5-10 minutes.

Stir the cocoa, sugar and water until the sugar dissolves. Take the pan off the heat and add icing sugar; beat well to a thick coating consistency. Decorate the top of the éclairs or buns while the icing is still warm. Fill with cream when cool.

Fruit Salad

SYRUP:
2 pints water
1 pound sugar
juice of 3 lemons
4 red-skinned apples, chopped into small squares
6 oranges (see p. 80)
1 melon, cut into squares or balls
3 bananas, sliced
2 fresh peaches, skinned and diced
8 ounces black grapes, halved and seeded
8 ounces green grapes, skinned and seeded

Make up the syrup by boiling the sugar in the water until it has dissolved. Add the strained lemon juice. Allow to cool. Prepare fruit. Add syrup and chill. Add the bananas and apples just before serving so that they do not brown.

Christmas Dinner

The traditional English Christmas dinner is one of the glories of our native cooking—if it is well done. This following menu is absolutely traditional. If this is the first Christmas dinner you have prepared make sure that you prepare as much as possible the day before so that you can enjoy it as much as the rest.

For 10 servings

GRAPEFRUIT & MELON COCKTAIL
ROAST TURKEY
  SAUSAGE STUFFING
  CHESTNUT STUFFING
  GIBLET GRAVY
  SAUSAGE and BACON ROLLS
  FRUIT RINGS
  CRANBERRY SAUCE
CHRISTMAS PUDDING
  BRANDY BUTTER
MINCE PIES

Grapefruit & Melon Cocktail

5 grapefruit (see p. 80 for
  preparation)
1 melon, cut into cubes
½ pint water
4 ounces sugar
10 maraschino cherries

Make up the syrup by boiling the water and sugar until it is dissolved. Allow to cool, add fruit. Arrange in dishes and put a cherry in the centre.

Roast Turkey

1 (12-pound) turkey
6 rashers bacon
salt and freshly ground black pepper

SAUSAGE STUFFING:
1 onion, finely chopped
butter
8 ounces sausage meat
2 tablespoons chopped parsley
2 eggs

juice of ½ lemon
thyme and marjoram
salt and freshly ground black pepper
8 ounces chicken livers, chopped
3 ounces dry breadcrumbs

Lightly sauté the onion in butter, add sausage meat and cook for about 3 minutes. Place in a bowl with the parsley, eggs, lemon juice, herbs and seasoning. Add the livers, add breadcrumbs and mix with the other ingredients and stuff the turkey.

Chestnut Stuffing

1 pound chestnuts
½ pint stock
3 ounces breadcrumbs
2 teaspoons parsley, chopped
1 ounce butter
1 teaspoon grated lemon rind
salt and pepper
1 egg

Slit the chestnut skins and boil in the stock for 10 minutes. Remove the skins and simmer gently in the stock until tender; about 40 minutes. Sieve, mix with breadcrumbs, parsley, butter, lemon rind and seasoning. Bind with beaten egg. Stuff this into the crop end of the turkey.

Now place the turkey in a roasting pan and cover the breast with rashers of bacon. Season and roast in a fairly hot oven, 400°F or Gas Mark 6, for 15 minutes. Reduce the temperature to 350°F, Gas Mark 3 and cook until the juices run clear when the leg is skewered. You need about 20 minutes for each pound. While cooking, baste often with lemon juice and melted butter.

If not golden enough when nearly cooked, roast for another 10 minutes at a higher heat, 425°F or Gas Mark 6.

If you are using a frozen turkey do remember to give it at least 18 hours to defrost. When you have to hurry the defrosting you tend to spoil the flavour.

Giblet Gravy

Turkey giblets
1 onion stuck with cloves
1½ pints water
bay leaf
6 peppercorns
sprig of parsley
2 ounces flour
salt and pepper
¼ pint red wine
juice of the turkey

Wash the giblets and put in a saucepan with the water, onion, bayleaf and peppercorns. Bring to the boil and simmer for at least 1-1½ hours. Allow to cool and strain the stock. When the turkey has been removed for carving, pour off the excess fat from the roasting tin and add the flour to the juice. Whisk then add the red wine and allow to bubble. Season and add giblet stock. A few drops of Soya sauce will give it a good colour. Keep warm until you serve.

Sausage and Bacon Rolls

20 Chipolata sausages
20 small rolls of bacon

Have the sausages pricked and the bacon rolled. Place prepared bacon and sausages on baking sheets then pop them in the oven 15-20 minutes before serving the turkey.

Garnish turkey with Sausage and Bacon Rolls when you serve.

Place turkey, legs to your right. First carve far side. Hold drumstick with fingers. Cut the joint joining the leg to the backbone.

Hold leg on plate. Cut joint to separate drumstick, thigh. Slice drumstick, turning for even slices. Slice the thigh parallel to bone.

To cut white meat, first make deep cut into breast to body frame, parallel to and close to wing. Anchor turkey with fork.

Starting halfway up breast, thinly slice white meat down to cut made above wing. Take stuffing from opening where leg was removed.

Fruit Rings

10 pineapple rings
10 peach halves
1 can cherries

Serve halved peaches sitting on pineapple rings filled with cherries. Heat in the oven. This is borrowed from an American Thanksgiving dinner and I have found it a popular addition to Christmas fare.

Cranberry Sauce

8 ounces sugar
½ pint water
8 ounces cranberries

Dissolve sugar in the water and boil for 5 minutes. Add cranberries and simmer for 10 minutes. Cool before serving. Add a little port for a really good flavour.

Christmas Pudding

For three 2-pint pudding basins

5 ounces plain flour
8 ounces fresh white breadcrumbs
½ teaspoon salt
½ teaspoon ground nuts
1 teaspoon mixed spice
4 ounces soft brown sugar
4 ounces granulated sugar
4 ounces shredded suet
4 ounces butter
8 ounces currants
8 ounces sultanas
8 ounces seeded raisins
4 ounces glacé cherries (halved)
2 ounces preserved ginger, chopped
4 ounces chopped almonds
4 ounces mixed peel, chopped
8 ounces peeled and grated apples
2 ounces carrots, finely grated
4 large eggs
2 tablespoons golden syrup
1 tablespoon black treacle
4 tablespoons brandy or sherry
8 tablespoons old ale or stout

Grease the basins and in the bottom of each place a round of greaseproof paper, brushed with melted fat. Put the first seven of the dry ingredients into a large mixing bowl, add the suet and rub in the butter. Warm the syrup and treacle and add them, together with the rest of the ingredients, mixing well. The mixture should be a dropping consistency but not runny. Fill the basins about three-quarters of the way up with the mixture. Cover with doubled rounds of greaseproof paper tied under the rims. Steam or boil the pudding, keeping the water constantly on the boil and replenishing the water from a boiling kettle. This will take 7-8 hours. If you make 1-pint puddings it will take about 4 hours.
Cool, remove coverings and replace with dry covers. Store in a cool, dry place. Before serving, steam for 2 hours then top with cream, custard or brandy butter (see below).
Try to make them at least 1 month before Christmas.

Brandy Butter

6 ounces unsalted butter
12 ounces icing sugar, sieved
3 tablespoons brandy

Cream butter until soft, add some icing sugar gradually, then brandy and remaining icing sugar.

Mince Pies

1 pound shortcrust pastry (see p. 9)
1½ pounds mincemeat

If you use bought mincemeat, add 1 tablespoon brandy or sherry before using.
Roll out the pastry thinly. Cut out with 2 different-sized scone cutters. Line patty tins with pastry; prick the bottoms. Put a teaspoon of mincemeat in each; wet edges of the bottom and top. Seal and pinch the edges. Cook for 10-15 minutes in a hot oven, 400°F or Gas Mark 6. Sprinkle with caster sugar while still hot.

Index

BASIC METHODS OF COOKING

BAKING—cooking in dry heat in the oven.

BOILING—cooking food in a boiling liquid (212°F), eg. vegetables, pasta and boiled puddings.

BRAISING—meat is browned then cooked slowly on a bed of vegetables with very little liquid, in a covered container.

FRYING—Shallow frying is cooking in just enough fat to cover the base of the pan. It is a quick method of cooking.
Deep frying is cooking food by immersing in a deep pan filled two-thirds full of hot fat or oil.

GRILLING—always pre-heat the grill for this method of cooking and brush the grill rack with fat. Food which is to be completely cooked by grilling should be cooked at a high temperature for the initial browning period. Then reduce the heat and complete the cooking.

POACHING—cooking food gently in liquid at simmering temperature (185-200°F).

POT ROASTING—a combination of frying and steaming. The meat is browned and then cooked in a heavy covered casserole or saucepan with fat only. It is a slow method of roasting and may be carried out on top of the stove or in the oven at a low temperature.

PRESSURE COOKING—cooking food at a very high temperature under pressure. The food cooks quickly and tougher types of meat are made more tender. Types of pressure cookers vary and the makers instructions should be followed explicitly.

ROASTING—cooking food at a high temperature in the oven. The container is open and little fat should be used.

SAUTÉ—To cook over a strong heat in a small amount of fat or oil, shaking the pan frequently to prevent sticking.

SIMMERING—cooking below boiling point—the liquid should bubble gently at the side of the pot.

STEAMING—using the steam from boiling water to cook food. The food may be cooked in a steamer over boiling water or the basin of food may be stood in the boiling water. Always cover the saucepan or steamer.

STEWING—cooking food at simmering point or below in a liquid. It is a long slow method of cooking and an excellent way of tenderising the tougher cuts of meat. Stewing is carried out in a covered container.

COOKING TERMS

BAIN MARIE—a roasting tin half filled with water in which a dish of food which must be baked slowly is placed before cooking in the oven, e.g. caramel custards.

BAKING BLIND—the method of baking flans, tarts and other pastry cases without a filling. Put the flan ring or pie dish on a baking sheet and line with pastry. Cut a circle of greaseproof paper slightly larger than the flan. Fill with dried beans, rice, or bread crusts to weigh the paper down. Bake the flan for 15 minutes. Remove the greaseproof paper and beans and bake a further 10 minutes to brown and crisp the pastry. Cool.

BASTING—spooning the cooking fat and liquid over food while roasting. This keeps the food moist, adds flavour and improves the appearance.

BEATING—method of introducing air to a mixture, a wooden spoon, wire whisk or electric beater may be used for this process.

BINDING—adding a liquid, egg or melted fat to a dry mixture to hold it together, e.g. beaten egg is added to mince for hamburgers.

BLANCHING—putting food in boiling water in order to either whiten, remove the skin, salt or strong flavour from food.

BLENDING—the process of mixing a thickening agent, such as flour or cornflour with a little cold water to a smooth paste. A little of the hot liquid to be thickened is then added to the paste and the whole returned to the saucepan. The mixture is stirred until it boils and thickens. Used to thicken the liquid of casseroles, stews and certain sauces.

BOUQUET GARNI—a bunch of fresh mixed herbs tied together with string and used for flavouring. Usually a bay leaf, sprig of parsley, sprig of thyme and perhaps a few celery leaves. Dried herbs may be used tied in a little muslin bag.

BROWNING—putting a cooked dish or meringue under the grill, or in the oven for a short time to give it an appetising golden colour.

CASSEROLE—baking dish usually ovenproof earthenware, pottery, porcelain or cast-iron with a tight fitting lid. Food cooked in a casserole is served straight from the dish.

CHINING—method of preparing neck or loin joints for easier carving. The bone at the wide end of the chops or cutlets is cut away from the meat so that it may be carved into portions of one rib each.

CHOPPING—dividing food into very small pieces on a chopping board using a very sharp knife.

COATING—covering food with a thin layer of flour, egg, breadcrumbs or batter before it is fried.

CONSISTENCY—term describing the texture (usually the thickness) of a mixture.

CREAMING—beating together fat and sugar to incorporate air, break down the sugar crystals and soften the fat.

FOLDING IN—to incorporate two mixtures using a light over and over motion. Usually applied to light mixtures such as whisked egg white or cream which have to be folded into other ingredients. It is important to carry out the process carefully so that the air is not knocked out of the light mixture. Flour is sifted over whisked egg mixtures for very light sponge cakes. The use of an electric mixer is not practical for this process. A sharp edged metal spoon is ideal for folding in.

GLAZE—a liquid brushed over the surface of a dish to give it a shiny finish.

GRATE—shaving food into shreds.

HULL—remove stalks from soft fruits—strawberries, raspberries etc.

KNEADING—working a dough using the fingertips for pastry-making and the knuckles for bread-making. The edges of the dough are drawn to the centre.

MARINADE—a liquid made of oil and wine, vinegar or lemon juice and flavouring vegetables, herbs and spices. Food is steeped in the marinade to tenderise and add flavour.

PURÉE—fresh or cooked fruit or vegetables are broken down into a smooth pulp by sieving, pounding or blending in the liquidiser.

REDUCING—boiling a liquid, uncovered, in order to evaporate the water content and make the liquid more concentrated.

ROUX—a thickening agent for soups and sauces. Equal quantities of fat and flour are cooked together.

RUBBING IN—a method of incorporating fat into flour, e.g. in short-crust pastry making. Add the fat in small pieces to the flour. Using the fingertips, quickly and lightly rub the fat into the flour, lifting the hands as you do this.

SEASONED FLOUR—mix 1 teaspoon of salt, a good sprinkling of pepper and 2 tablespoons flour. Use to coat food before cooking.

SIEVING—to rub food through a sieve using a wooden spoon, in order to discard skin, stalks or seeds.

SKIMMING—to remove the scum or fat from food whilst it is cooking. A piece of absorbent kitchen paper or a metal spoon are used.

STOCK—a well-flavoured liquid made by simmering meat and/or vegetables in water for a prolonged period, to extract the flavour. When time is short the commercial stock cubes may be substituted.

SWEATING—cooking foods, usually vegetables in a small amount of fat to soften and add flavour. The pan is always covered.

WATER BATH—see Bain marie.

WHIPPING OR WHISKING—adding air quickly to a mixture by beating with a hand whisk, rotary beater or electric beater.

ZEST—the thin coloured skin of citrus fruit which contains the oil and flavour.